Praise for Saturda~

"There are hundreds of books about football! Books about the players, books about the games, books about the coaches, books about the fans.

"Ever read a book about officials? I thought so. We moan, complain, criticize, and scream . . . about what? About officials, that's what! And we know nothing about them.

"Ever wonder what officials are thinking? I certainly have, and now we can know for sure. Gus Morris has written a delightful book about the challenging, disturbing, sad, hilarious world of football officiating. If you love football, read this book—at last you will understand the strange world of officials, and you might even come to like them.

"One thing is certain: you will love Gus Morris!"

—*Bill Curry*
Former player, coach, speaker

"During the evaluation process, there were multiple positive comments to consider; however, perhaps the most important word that was repeated in reference to Gus was integrity. Every official knows the broad and all-encompassing meaning of the word. Without integrity, you cannot be of the quality a Southeastern Conference official is required to be.

"Time after time, Gus has performed on and off the field in the manner befitting an SEC football official and with tremendous pride in his work. What he has, and continues to bring to the world of officiating through his work with young guys wanting to be a part of the SEC family, will contribute to a great group of officials."

—*Bobby Gaston*
Former coordinator of SEC Football Officials

"What sets Gus's book apart is it is a day in the life of a great college official. It is not only about sports but also about life—Gus's life—and it has something for everyone.

"If you only buy one book this year, this is the one you will enjoy most, from getting up four hours early to go to a clinic to stories that just happened to be told during the football season, you can't make this stuff up.

"I highly recommend this as a great gift and a great read."

— **Dr. Jack Kelly**
Official, mentor, business coach

"Having worked with Gus on the field in the SEC for several years, we can tell you that it was never boring with Gus Morris! His ability to work with coaches on the sideline was second to none. The line of scrimmage guys always get the brunt of the coaches' wrath when the calls do not go their way. Gus was a master at this. We can all remember several times where a coach is in the middle of a tirade and Gus was totally stoic, with no emotion whatsoever. And then on the next time out, you would look over at him and he'd give you that smile like, 'I got this handled over here, no worries.' And when a coach crossed the line, he would always make sure he would gently throw that flag directly between the feet of the coach. No emotion, no excitement. Gus always liked to keep a list of all the coaches he had worked in front of. And the list would get longer and longer every year. He took a lot of joy in that, and rightfully so.

"As most officials will tell you, the games themselves are a small part of what we call the football officiating life—three to four hours out of the weekend. During these football weekends, you learn so much of what your crewmates are all about. Gus was a great crewmate. He was always quick to inject some humor into our meetings. Always offering up a funny picture or video to any prospective victims we had on the crew that week. And when he was called upon to help, the meals he provided the crew on Friday nights were always incredible! That guy is quite the grill and fry cook!

"Gus has a long history of involvement with the SEC through his years of service, and of course, being the son of an SEC official. Officiating over that last several years has evolved. It is a thankless job, and the scrutiny is endless. Some officials struggle with this. Gus was

truly an old-school official who never let things on the field take the enjoyment out of the avocation. Good or bad, Gus was always smiling.

"It was our privilege to know and work with Gus Morris."

—Jesse Dupuy, Matt Loeffler, Mike Shirey, Stan Weihe, and Bobby Ables
SEC crew members

"Gus Morris has captured and created a picture of how these friendships create the "best team" on the field! Gus, in a series of short stories, shows you how hard we work, laugh, hug, and often anguish, hurt, and cry.

"Gus has been the ultimate teammate and friend to hundreds of officials at all levels of officiating. After reading this book, you will understand why he is a great ambassador for football officiating and why he is loved by all. I am proud to call him my lifetime friend and teammate!

"This is a story about life in the SEC!"

—Chris Conley
Former official, chaplain, home builder

Saturdays
in the
South

Saturdays in the South

A Collection of Stories from My Thirty-One Years of

Officiating Football in the Southeastern Conference

G. A. "Gus" Morris III

BOOKLOGIX

Alpharetta, Georgia

ISBN: 978-1-6653-0563-1 - Paperback
eISBN: 978-1-6653-0564-8 - ePub

⊗This paper meets the requirements of ANSI/NISO Z39.48-1992 (Permanence of Paper)

0 3 0 1 2 3

*This book is dedicated to my mother and father
who brought me into this world.*

To my four sisters who taught me more than I ever realized.

To Jack Kelly and Ron Goings for teaching me how to officiate football.

*To Bobby Gaston for taking a chance on me and making me a part of
the Southeastern Conference Football Officials Association.*

*To the countless men I worked with over the years
that became the brothers that I never had.*

*And especially, my children, August and Susan. Like the early
relationship with my father, I was not around very much.*

Contents

Foreword

For the past forty-six years it has been my good fortune to cover college football for newspapers, radio, television, and the internet. It has been an incredible journey that has allowed me to make friends that will last a lifetime and stay close to a game that I fell in love with when I was thirteen years old.

And here's what I know: college football officials are the least-understood and least-appreciated people who work in the game.

Until now.

When Gus Morris shared with me his notes for this book, I knew exactly what it was going to be. Like the man who wrote it, the book is an inside look at college football officiating that pulls no punches. Gus gives it to us straight because that's the only way he knows how to do it.

As he pulls back the curtain and lets us into his world, we learn that college football officiating isn't a part-time job or a hobby. It is a lifestyle. And you choose this lifestyle knowing there will be good times, not-so-good times, and yes, painful times along the way. The buy-in has to be complete.

This book will make you laugh:

- Like the time a coach from UT-Chattanooga pleaded for help when he was getting his brains kicked in by Auburn. Gus responded, "Coach, I'm helping you all I can, but I need a little more effort from your guys." Auburn won, 62–24.
- Or the time that the head coach from Northeast Louisiana gave him a tip right before the opening kickoff: "We're going to onside kick." Gus made sure he was in perfect position for the onside kick, which was recovered by Northeast Louisiana. Gus was right on top of the call and made it with enthusiasm. There was only one problem: he pointed the wrong way.
- Or the time a smart-aleck lower-level assistant from LSU kept giving Gus a hard time. Gus asked for the guy's name, explaining that when he threw the unsportsmanlike-conduct flag that was surely coming, he would be able to give Head Coach Les Miles the fellow's name. Gus didn't hear a peep from the guy the rest of the game.

But there are also moments in the book that pull on your heart strings:

- Gus is the son of the late George Morris, a Hall of Fame football player at Georgia Tech and a long-time college official. George did a lot of traveling when Gus was a boy, so they didn't spend a lot of time together. When Gus made it as an official in the SEC, the two had lunch. George gave Gus his SEC officiating ring and insisted that he wear it now. "You've earned it," said George. When George Morris died on December 10, 2007, Gus attended two funeral services—one in Atlanta and another in George's native Vicksburg, Mississippi, where he was laid to rest. Gus held it together emotionally until he arrived back at his home in Cumming, Georgia. There, near the driveway, was a neat pile of firewood given to him by Chris Conley, one of his best friends in officiating. Attached was a note: *"Careful. Wood soaked in kerosene. Love, Santa."* That's when he lost it.

- At the Alabama-Auburn game in 1996 in Tuscaloosa, Gus and Coach Gene Stallings attended to a member of the Alabama drill team who was accidently knocked to the ground by a member of the band. Coach Stallings held the girl's hand, brushed away her tears, and assured her it was going to be okay. He and Gus did not allow the game to start until she was able to walk off the field.

- "Gus, do you know how lucky we are to be doing this?" Coach Stallings asked.

- As the final seconds of the game wound down, Gus passed by Coach Stallings one last time. The Alabama coach stuck out his hand. "I'm done," he said. After the game—a 24–23 win by Alabama—Gene Stallings resigned as Alabama's head coach after seven seasons.

There is some pain:

- One night in Columbia, South Carolina, Gus took a direct hit from two players at once. He had to be removed from the field. He suffered a severe concussion. It took him nine months to fully recover.

- More than once he found it difficult to get out of bed on Sunday morning because of a hit he took the day before. It comes with the job.

And he had to be flexible:

- Once during a game, fellow official Steve Shaw had the pocket ripped off of his officiating shirt after an on-field collision. At halftime, Gus managed to get his hands on a needle and some black thread. His great aunt taught him to sew as a boy. Problem solved.

There is so much more to be found within the covers of this book. And when you finish, I'll make this one promise: you will never look at college football officials the same way again. Will you still cuss their names when a call goes against your favorite team? Of course. Gus Morris wouldn't have it any other way.

—Tony Barnhart

Tony Barnhart was a college football writer with the Atlanta Journal-Constitution *for twenty-five years (1984–2008). He has also worked for ESPN, CBS Sports, and the SEC Network. He is a member of the Georgia Sports Hall of Fame.*

Introduction

The epicenter of college football resides in the Southeastern Conference. Even though most won't openly admit it, fans from outside the footprint of the South know this to be an undeniable fact.

What makes SEC football so great is a combination of many unique ingredients: Tradition should be put at the top of the list. The legendary coaches and players certainly formed the foundation for the league. The overall talent level of the athletes is beyond anything found in other conferences. The atmosphere surrounding the stadiums is intimidating and electrifying. And the game-day passion of the fans borders on cult-like behavior.

But there's one element that rarely gets discussed, except when something appears to go wrong in the eyes of the fans. The one critical part of the game that is taken for granted consists of the group of individuals that are charged with the responsibility of applying the rules fairly and impartially—the officials. For without them, the game as we know it couldn't exist. The majority of fans have no idea who the officials are or where they are from.

Only a handful of people knew what I did on the weekends when I left home. The jobs that I held and the businesses

I owned didn't bank on them knowing. When they did become aware, they were surprised and amazed: "Wow, I've never met a SEC official." I don't know what they were expecting but it obviously wasn't what was standing in front of them.

I grew up in a sports-oriented family. My father, George Morris, was an academic All-American at Georgia Tech in the late 1940s and early '50s. He also had a short pro career with the San Francisco 49ers. He began officiating football in the Southeastern Conference the year after I was born, 1960. My four sisters played basketball, softball, or were cheerleaders at some point in their youth. My mother made sure we got to where we were supposed to be and on time.

While growing up, I was kept busy playing recreational league football, baseball, gymnastics, and judo. I played football and wrestled at Marist High School in Atlanta. From there, I went on to play football at Millsaps College.

After graduating from Millsaps in 1982, I worked at UPS for three years before moving back to Atlanta to attend graduate school at Georgia Tech and work part time. Wanting to stay active and to have something fun to do, I joined a softball league; I had played softball in Mississippi after college and really enjoyed it. But the Atlanta league was not for me. I had competed all my life. I was just looking for something to do in my spare time. There were enough physical altercations between the teams that made me realize I was in the wrong place.

While I was at work one afternoon, a friend of mine stopped by to see me. As he was leaving, I walked with him to his car. I noticed a black-and-white-striped shirt hanging in the back-seat area. I knew what it was from having seen my father's. He mentioned that there was a high school officials' meeting that evening. He then asked me if I would be interested in attending. Still wanting to do something fun and remain active, I said, "Yes," and I met up with him later that day.

Not long after the meeting got under way, I realized that this was something I should at least try. I registered, started studying the rules, bought a uniform, and prepared to officiate my first football game. Five weeks later, I did just that on the morning of Saturday, September 13, 1986. It was a game between seventh and eighth graders at Marietta High School, located just north of Atlanta. I was really concerned that I didn't know the rules well enough. I spoke to the referee about this, and he said to just call what is obvious, don't go looking for anything. Once the game started, I felt comfortable but two things immediately became clear: One, I didn't have a mouthpiece in. And two, I wasn't looking through a facemask. It's funny what you can take for granted during your playing career. I certainly knew the game from a player's perspective, and this helped me as the game progressed. When the game was over, I thought to myself, "I can do this!"

Over the next five seasons, with the help of many important people, I had developed into a pretty good football official. Actually, good enough to start working assignments with the Southeastern Conference. The interesting thing about all of this is that I was still just doing it for something fun to do in my spare time. Little did I know about the journey I was about to embark on.

Most fans don't realize what officials never experience: There's no celebration of great plays, officials don't win or lose, confetti doesn't fall from the sky when a game is officiated correctly, and there are no post-game award presentations. After the last whistle, the men in stripes go back home and carry on with their normal life.

Throughout my career as an SEC football official, I made hundreds of speeches to all types of organizations. I discovered early on that providing more time for questions and answers created the best experience for the audiences. Quoting statistics and mundane rule language was boring.

During those presentations, I heard over and over that I should write a book. Because I was still working on the field as an active official, it was absolutely inappropriate for me to do so.

I held firmly to the belief that I shouldn't and wouldn't talk openly about coaches, specific games that I was involved in, or how teams performed during their practices, etc. I also made sure I was never seen as a "fan" at any game I attended in my spare time. I wanted my reputation to remain that of impartiality. I never posted anything about officiating on social media until after I retired from the field.

After thirty-one years, my time as an SEC official had run its course. It was time for me to step aside and give someone else the opportunity to experience what I had. Shortly after my retirement, I was persuaded by a friend to begin compiling an inventory of bullet points that would help me recall my experiences. For a year and a half, I composed a list of happenings. The pages in this book contain many short stories from that list that chronical my time working my way through all the years of officiating in the Southeastern Conference.

The best advice I got in regard to officiating was to get there early and don't be in a rush to leave after the game. Fortunately, I was smart enough to do just that. Had I not, I wouldn't have been able to keep everything in perspective and have the experiences that I did. I also learned not to take myself too seriously. Because of this, I was always able to do it for enjoyment and to stay active. And this enabled me to put together a very entertaining collection of stories.

Like all books, there is a first page and a last page. However, this book is not laid out in a structured, chronological order. You can open it to any page and start reading. No story depends on the previous one for understanding. Within some stories, there are references to others only to provide additional insight.

If you enjoy sports or have a curiosity about the men in

stripes, you are in for an interesting read. My hope is there will be a new perspective of those that are responsible for managing the games you are so passionate about. Enjoy! Oh yeah, my daughter's wedding is coming soon, and I want to help pay for that!

Walk the Line

CHAIN CREWS

The position that I worked throughout my entire career with the SEC was that of a head linesman. Part of my responsibilities was to coordinate the activities of the chain crew. Those are the people that operate the equipment on the sidelines that indicate downs and distances. These people come from all walks of life.

Being a member of an SEC chain crew is almost treated as a lifetime appointment. When a member retires, he generally designates his replacement. Within the chain crew resides an assortment of challenging personality types. Most are great people, but there are those few that are a real pain in the ass to deal with. Some of them know everything there is to know, and they want to do it their way. Or they want to do it the way it's been done for the last fifty years.

It is the responsibility of the linesman and line judge to have a pregame meeting with the chain crew at the stadium about an hour and forty-five minutes prior to kick-off. The linesman usually conducts the meeting, offering the line judge to add anything at the end that may have been overlooked.

The Southeastern Conference Football Officials Association would spend many hours going over how we wanted the chain crews to work during our preseason clinic in July. We also coordinated how we, as head linesmen, were going to do certain things before, during, and after the game. It amazed me the number of times where I would conduct the pregame and how many times I would hear, "Well, that's not what the guy wanted us to do last Saturday." Ugh!

I was involved in well over three hundred pregame meetings and I always started them off by thanking the chain crew for their help and reminding them that they were just as critical an element for the game as the officials. My routine was the same week in and week out: I followed the normal course of things that would happen in a game. I emphasized that they pay attention to the coin toss, which let them know the correct end of the field to line up on. We discussed how we would move the chains on first downs. They were reminded to not get in a hurry or move too quickly. We talked about what to look out for on punts and field goals. The pregame meeting usually lasted about fifteen minutes.

Most of the time, the members of the chain crew were willing to do whatever was asked of them. But again, you had those few who just wanted to do it their way. The goal was to have a proficient chain crew who could navigate the challenges that may occur during the game, get out of the game without being noticed. I would bend a little and adjust to some of these personalities when necessary. Some of these people were big-time boosters and they just thought they ruled the roost. Whatever!

There were some chain crews that took great pride in how they performed during the game. Ole Miss consistently had one of the best chain crews on a yearly basis. Texas A&M, Tennessee, LSU, Auburn (less the play-clock operator), Alabama, and Georgia were usually pretty good. Missouri, South Carolina, Mississippi State, Arkansas, and Vanderbilt were okay. Then you had the bottom of the heap, in my opinion: Florida and Kentucky.

Speaking of Florida, I had a game there in 2017, I think— LSU at Florida. CBS televised it with a 3:30 prime-time kick-off. It was ten degrees cooler on the field at kickoff than it was the previous week during the same time slot in Baton Rouge. Still, it was 107 degrees on the field. We had our normal pregame meeting with the always challenging Florida-based chain crew. There was one guy who always seemed to be the fly in the ointment. I've had several problems with him over the years. He seemed like the ringleader. One thing I always emphasize during every pregame meeting is to be ready for the second-half kickoff and to know which end of the field the ball will be kicked to.

In this game, the teams and the game officials are out on the field for warm-ups, getting ready for the second half. The halftime clock is counting down with two minutes remaining—no chain crew. One minute—no chain crew. I'm looking toward the tunnel where the chain crew will come out—no chain crew. The crew breaks our mid-field huddle to start the second half—no chain crew. We get lined up in our kickoff positions—no chain crew. The Red Hat starts leaving the field indicating that we are ready to go—no chain crew. I now must shut everything down so the game doesn't start and physically go get the chain crew out of their locker room.

There was absolutely no sense of urgency on their part. Some were still in the men's room. I used words you never, ever hear in church. After delaying the start of the game for almost three minutes because the chain crew was so out of sync, my second-half interaction with them was rather frosty. They knew that they had really screwed up and it could cost them their position on the chain crew. How much money is on the line with CBS putting the game in their primetime slot and maybe forty million eyeballs watching the game? This was a major, major deal.

After that situation, the Southeastern Conference began evaluating each member institution chain crew. The ranking list was shared with the chain crews around the league. Not much really changed because of that, particularly at Florida.

Back around 1995 or so, I had the Vanderbilt at Florida game. It had the feel of a game pitting men against boys. Steve Spurrier had Florida rolling and Vanderbilt was turning coaches over just about every other year. I believe Woody Wodenhoufer was the coach at Vanderbilt. Florida could have scored a 100 but called off the dogs, or gators if you're so inclined, in the second half.

In the second quarter, somehow, Florida got themselves in a fourth and short situation on about the fifty-yard line and decided to go for it. Of course, they make it. Mr. "Fly in the Ointment" decides to celebrate, as a chain crew member, in the Florida team area, and exclaims that "Florida never misses when they go for it on fourth down." I glare toward him, and he's got his clipboard, used for charting fouls, wedged between his right forearm and his fat right hip. On the back of the clipboard are three Florida Gator logo stickers. Wodenhoufer is pissed. I'm pissed.

When we get to the locker room for halftime, I asked the cop that escorts us to and from the stadium to go out to our van and retrieve my clipboard. He was back lickety split. I asked Bill Goss, our referee, to come with me. I asked "Mr. Fly in the Ointment" to come out of the chain crew locker room for a chat and to bring his clipboard with him. I got on his ass hard about his behavior on the sideline and how it was going to get me killed. I took his clipboard and flung it across the hall, smashing it against the wall. I then handed him my own personal clipboard that I normally give the chain crew to use during the game. I offered this same clipboard to "Mr. Fly in the Ointment" during our pregame meeting, but *no*, he told me he had his own clipboard that he wanted to use, and I didn't need to give him mine. This worked out horribly. Lesson learned: my clipboard was used at Florida from then on. With the meeting over, Bill and I walked back to our locker room. Bill, in his unique voice, asked, "Do you think you were a little hard on him?" My reply was "F@*k him!" Bill then says, "Guess not."

Speaking of chain crews, in my early years of officiating, I worked many games at Georgia Southern in Statesboro, Georgia. This was during the Erk Russell era. The chain crew at Georgia Southern boasted about being the smartest chain crew in America. You see, each member of the crew had a doctorate degree. They were an amazingly fun group of guys to be involved with.

Another memorable chain crew incident happened in 2005 during the Tennessee at Notre Dame game. With three minutes and twelve seconds left to go in the third quarter, I had a flag down for a late hit out of bounds against Notre Dame. Yes, it was a close call and could have gone either way except for the fact that the defensive back went low into the left knee of the running back. If it had been at the hips or higher, I might not have called it.

During the dead ball period, things were moving right along. I've relayed the foul information to Steve Shaw, our referee. We begin administering the penalty when suddenly, the box man on the chain crew, who I communicate with on every play, tells me "That was a bullshit call!" We are standing in the Tennessee team area.

My first thought was, at all costs, avoid a chain crew mutiny! My second thought was my brother-in-law, sister, and wife are in the stands—I could quickly train them and get them to work the chains for the rest of the game. Instead, I used my honed people skills and got right up in his face so that I didn't have to talk loudly. We had what is referred to as a "come to Jesus" meeting. Being that the game was at Notre Dame, I thought it was appropriate. I could sense early in my discussion that he knew he had said something he shouldn't have. NBC caught the whole interaction and broadcast it to the world, without sound. So much for being subtle. We finished the game without any additional friction; Notre Dame won. The chain crew was happy, I guess. As was customary with every chain crew I worked with, I shook each member's hand and thanked them for their work that day.

About five months later, I'm working a spring scrimmage in Knoxville, Tennessee. Everyone was on the field in Neyland Stadium waiting for the practice to get started.

Coach Fulmer and several assistants walk over to me. I'm like, *What is this all about?* Coach Fulmer shakes my hand and says he and his coaches enjoyed watching me handle the chain crew guy at Notre Dame. My response was, "Y'all saw that?" One of his assistants replied, "Hell, how could we not? You were right in our team area." I had no idea due to me being totally focused on the guy and trying to avoid a mutiny.

STANDING ALL ALONE

In officiating, it's not a matter of if, it's a matter of when. Every official is going to miss a call that should have been made or make a call that should have been left alone. Such was the case for me on November 19, 2011.

Occasionally, Tennessee and Vanderbilt will play a great game against one another. James Franklin, who was the head coach of the Commodores, had developed his team into a formidable opponent for any team.

Tennessee was in its second year with Derek Dooley as their coach. The Volunteers were at the beginning of a long spiral of being a dumpster fire of a team. The Lane Kiffen show had lasted only one year before he bolted to the West Coast. Dooley came over from Louisiana Tech and just didn't seem to be a good fit at Tennessee. Up next was Butch Jones.

Jones had a good run at Cincinnati before coming to Knoxville. The 2017 season spelled doom for him. Jeremy Pruitt, a Nick Saban protégé, was next up. He was supposed to save the Volunteers. This hire was controversial and included changes with the athletics director. The internal conflict within the athletic department at Tennessee was at fever pitch.

At the time of this writing, Josh Heupel is the head ball coach. Maybe he can at least provide some stability and turn things around for the Volunteers.

I mention these coaches because during this period in the history of the games played between Vandy and Tennessee, the Commodores were batting about .500 against the Volunteers. They felt like they could line up and play with them every year.

9

The game in 2011 was no different. Because it was a night game, I drove to Knoxville on that Saturday morning. I arrived a little before noon so that I could join my crew for lunch. The weather was perfect for an evening kickoff.

The game was evenly matched and competitive. At the end of the first half, Tennessee was only up 14 to 7. At the end of regulation, the game was tied at 21 apiece and headed to overtime.

The Volunteers won the toss to begin overtime and elected to go on defense. Vanderbilt started on offense from the Tennessee twenty-five-yard line in the north end of the endzone. Jordan Rodgers ran for ten yards and a Vandy first down at the fifteen. The next play gained zero yards. On second down, they picked up four yards off a Zac Stacy run and had the ball on the eleven-yard line. On third down, Rodgers dropped back to pass, and the ball was intercepted by Eric Gordan, a freshman from the Nashville area. This is where "the matter of when" happened for me.

When the ball was intercepted, Neyland Stadium exploded. The noise was deafening. No one on the field heard my whistle. Everybody, players and officials, ran eighty-eight yards to the other end of the field for an apparent touchdown. Everyone except for me. Frantically blowing my whistle, I finally got the attention of my other crew members. I was standing on the opposite end of the field on the twelve-yard line, alone. All alone. I had ruled Eric Gordon down when he intercepted the ball.

When all the officials returned to the other end of the field, I explained to the referee that the ball had been intercepted but the player's knee was touching the ground when he caught it. It would be Tennessee's ball at the twenty-five-yard line.

While this is going on, the play is being shown on the stadium's jumbotron. The first angle looks okay but then there is a replay from a different angle coming from a camera in the north end of the stadium. The stadium erupts. I immediately knew something was wrong. This view shows that the player's knee was about an inch and a half from the ground. He was not down. I had blown the call. Neyland Stadium never seemed so large to me. I wanted to be anywhere else besides where I was standing at that moment. I had failed as an official, in the worst way.

As we were setting up for the second possession of the first overtime series, our pagers go off indicating that the previous play is under further review. Because I had ruled the ball dead, it shouldn't have been a reviewable play. However, the replay official made the decision that he hadn't heard a whistle. He overturned the call and ruled it a touchdown. Tennessee won the game on a walk-off touchdown, 27–21. I didn't remember if I blew my whistle or not immediately after the interception, but I damn sure remember signaling the ball dead and waving my arms.

When we get back to the hotel, there's no question that I blew the call. Going into the postgame debriefing was excruciating. I had never been so embarrassed in my officiating career. I wasn't getting much support from my crewmates. I had let them down and caused embarrassment for them as well.

The entire postgame meeting focused on this one play: Steve Shaw and the collaborative replay staff in Birmingham are on the phone. The replay official is explaining how he got to the decision he made. Yes, there was a whistle from me. You can hear it as plain as day during the replay on the TV broadcast. Again, there never should have been a replay. Mike Pereira, a football rules expert, said Replay and I should have been fired. Probably so, and it would have been justified.

Mike had been an official and to hear these words come from his mouth was very hard to take. I considered him a friend and ally.

I was sick about the entire situation.

The side judge and I were splitting a room that weekend. After our postgame meeting, we went up to the room. I started packing my gear away in my bag. I told him, "I'm going home, I won't be able to sleep for a while." He completely understood. He offered as much support as he could and told me to be careful driving home. It was shortly after midnight when I walked out of the hotel.

I thought about the play repeatedly during the drive home. While driving about five miles south of the I-75 and I-24 split in Chattanooga, my cell phone rings. When I answer, it was the personal assistant for Steve Shaw, the coordinator of football officiating.

"I figured you were up, so I thought I would give you a call." She knew I was hurting. Of all the people that could have called, she was the only one that did. When we finished talking, I was very appreciative. She understood, being that I was one of the men she helped oversee.

I pulled into my driveway around 3:45 in the morning. I was tired but still couldn't sleep. I poured a scotch, neat, and sat on my front porch in the dark, alone.

I realized that no matter what happened, the last play of the last game of that regular season was going to be the worst play of my officiating career. It was up to me to work through it. And I did. For nine more seasons.

If you ever want to feel small, really small, go stand on the twelve-yard line of the field in Neyland Stadium, alone. You'll realize what perspective is all about.

OFFICIALS' SECURITY DETAIL

When a crowd of eighty to a hundred thousand people start booing the officials, you begin to realize that you are seriously outnumbered. Sun Tzu would have a tough time figuring out how to prevail in a predicament of this magnitude.

There's a reason why Southeastern Conference officials are transported to and from the stadiums the way they are. In the words of Everett Kennard from Mississippi State, "There's crazy people out there!"

The game officials all meet in one room at the hotel where they stay during game weekend. Everyone is dressed in their uniform and ready to go. It allows for one more check to make sure you have everything you need. When it's time to leave for the stadium, the officials all leave together and go straight to the waiting van. These vans are usually driven by individuals associated with the schools. However, there are a couple of places where law enforcement does the driving.

The drive to the stadium is done under police escort with rolling roadblocks. These drives can be intense. There's no mistake, as the convoy gets close to the stadium, for fans to realize that the officials are arriving.

Upon arrival at the stadium, the officials are brought into a gated area, separated from "crazy people," where they unload and go straight to the dressing room. Exposure to the crowds is minimized to prevent problems.

At the end of the first half of play and the conclusion of the game, every official runs to one area of the field. There is an entourage of law enforcement waiting for the crew. This occurs to make sure the officials are safely escorted to the locker for halftime or the vans for the trip back to the hotel after the game. More often than not, the officials are back in their rooms showering before most fans have left the stadium.

The plan didn't play out the way it was designed back on September 18, 1999. Alabama was struggling under the leadership of Mike Dubose. The Crimson Tide had won their first two games of the season. The next game was in Birmingham, at Legion Field, against Louisiana Tech. Alabama couldn't get into any sort of rhythm. There were numerous procedural fouls during the game—false starts, illegal formations, offsides, etc. Frustration was apparent in their team area.

With two seconds left on the game clock, concluding an eighty-yard drive, Louisiana Tech's walk-on quarterback, Brian Stallworth, threw a desperation pass into the end zone. It was caught by Sean Cangelosi to tie the game at 28-all. With no time left, Tech made the extra point for a walk-off upset against Alabama.

As the crew was running to the designated rendezvous point, members of the Alabama State Patrol began running slightly ahead of us. It resembled a well-rehearsed relay team. Just as we entered the tunnel to leave the stadium, three Alabama fans jumped over the security fencing. Fortunately, I could see what was unfolding due to me leading the pack. I was able to avoid a swing by one of the gentlemen. "Don't stop!" came from the trooper directly in front of me. Our back judge wasn't so lucky. He caught a shot right to the mouth, but he didn't go down. The same cannot be said about the three brainless wonders that decided to break the rules. They were on the ground, in handcuffs, before we reached the van parked outside the stadium.

This was a serious situation. The conference office knew it

was. People in charge studied what transpired and made changes. Fortunately, it hasn't happened again. Yet.

I never found out what happened to those guys. The back judge was called to testify at a hearing in Birmingham several months later. After the way the troopers laid into them, I don't know if any further punishment was necessary.

THE MILE-
AND-A-HALF RUN

In 1992, the Southeastern Conference supervisor of officials, Bobby Gaston, implemented the timed mile-and-a-half run as part of the preseason clinic held annually in Birmingham, Alabama. Coaches around the leagues had been voicing concerns that there were officials that were not able to perform at a high level for the entirety of their games. Bobby consulted with Rod Walters from the University of South Carolina, and they determined that this distance was a good indicator of the physical conditioning of an official. It was often said that anyone could run a mile, but the extra half mile was very telling.

Groups of ten or twelve officials would run at a time. In the beginning, each group was made up of a single position. For example, the referees all ran together. One thing that became apparent from the start was that the younger guys were finishing well ahead of the rest of the field. After a little tweaking over the next few years, the groups were formed using the ages of the members. The older officials would run first, earlier in the morning, usually starting around 6:15. The last group of younger officials wouldn't begin their run until around 9:30 or later. The temperature in Birmingham could rise ten degrees or more over that time frame. Regardless of the temperature, the humidity was always hovering around 80 to 90 percent.

There were some guys who didn't complete the run in their required time and some that were not able to finish it.

One year, a hotshot first-year official started the run, made two laps around the track, ran through the gate to the parking lot, got in his car, and left. He was never seen again. I guess his heart wasn't in it for officiating in the Southeastern Conference.

If an individual didn't complete the run in their prescribed time, they had additional opportunities at conference member schools. It never ceased to amaze me how many guys could suddenly gain three or four minutes when they ran at their alma mater.

For all intents and purposes, the clinic was over after completing the run for most officials. The rules test was usually administered the night before. So, the rest of the meetings were just talk with short beer breaks during the day.

One consistent ritual that occurred every year right after completing the run was to hurry and get cleaned up back at the hotel. Then there was a caravan to Dreamland Bar-B-Que. There's nothing like half a slab of ribs and three or four beers on an empty stomach. Particularly on a Friday morning around eleven.

Having a nice buzz and a full belly created an insurmountable challenge of staying awake, listening to the steady droning of monotonous speakers, during early-afternoon group and breakout sessions.

The last time the mile-and-a-half requirement was enforced was in July of 2019. The following year, the summer preseason clinic was held virtually. On the morning of July 24, 2020, I got dressed in my running clothes and shoes. I drove up to Forsyth Central High School, climbed under the locked gate, and ran my mile and a half. It wasn't my fastest time, but it had been a ritual for the previous twenty-eight years. I figured, why not for old time's sake? Over the entire time that the mile-and-a-half run was required, it never rained!

In total, I covered forty-three-and-a-half miles during the

physical-assessment part of the preseason clinic. I may not have been able to officiate to the level of some people's expectations, but I could sure run like a son of bitch.

I SHOULD HAVE WORN SOME SHOES

In late July of 2000, my daughter, Susan, and I spent the day at Lake Lanier Islands water park. The previous several days had been really hot and this day was no different. It would be nice to spend time together and go somewhere to get some relief from the heat of summer.

We went on a Wednesday, just after lunch time. The drive to the park was about forty minutes from the house. We took only what we would need inside the park—towels, sunscreen, and some cash. We didn't want to be lugging around a bunch of stuff.

I parked the car in what little bit of shade I could find. It was not a short walk across the parking lot to the entrance but at least the car was not in the direct sun. Susan and I walked across the parking lot and paid to get in. She waited by the entrance while I walked back to the car to lock up my wallet and hide my keys. Because we were going to be in the water most of the time, I thought it made sense to leave my shoes in the car. Everything was set.

The distance across the parking lot was about seventy-five yards. About a third of the way across, I realized I was in trouble. The black asphalt was incredibly hot. My feet were on fire. I either had to keep going or return to the car for my shoes. I focused on the entrance, where Susan was waiting on me. I tightroped the white lines as best I could to stay off the black inferno.

Everything inside the water park was light-colored cement so the surface temperature was tolerable. My feet were a little uncomfortable but being in the water provided much relief. We enjoyed the park for about six hours and left for home at about seven o'clock. We were both pretty tired from having done just about everything there was to do.

The next day, I had to leave for Birmingham, Alabama, to attend the SEC summer preseason clinic. When I woke up that morning, I realized that my feet had some serious blisters on the bottom of them. My feet hurt no matter what shoes I put on. I ended up wearing a pair of well-worn loafers. They were not my best-looking shoes, but they hurt my feet the least of any others.

Friday morning was when the official's physical assessment was completed. Part of the evaluation requires everyone to run a timed mile and a half.

I had multiple quarter-sized blisters on both feet, but I was going to run the mile and a half no matter what. There are several athletic trainers from multiple conference member schools to administer the physical assessments. They perform blood-pressure tests, monitor the officials as they go through the various tests, and record the results for use by the coordinator of officials.

I made a couple of the trainers aware of the condition of my feet. They told me to get up on one of the training tables and remove my shoes and socks. They then taped small, foam donuts over each blister. When they were done, I put my socks and shoes back on.

Now I had a different discomfort. The blisters were not in direct contact with the bottom of my shoes but walking on the donuts was far from anything comfortable.

I completed the run under the required time but well over what I was normally capable of. The whole time I was running, all I could think of was the blazing hot parking lot and how foolish it was of me to think leaving my shoes in the car was a good idea. Each lap seemed to get longer and longer. When I finally crossed the finish line, I felt relief like I had never experienced before.

It took a little over a week for the blisters to heal. No matter how much trouble it may be, I will always wear my shoes to the water park.

7-4-2-b

The start of the pregame meeting is determined by the scheduled time for the kickoff of the game. For instance, if it's an evening game, the pregame meeting is usually scheduled for midmorning and continues to around noon.

When the start time is eleven a.m. central time, the pregame meeting will either be completed Friday evening and split up with it being finished Saturday early morning.

Friday meetings can be a mental challenge. For most officials, traveling to the game begins with making sure that work-related issues are addressed and taken care of. Then, the actual travel begins. You either start driving or you go to an airport. When flying to a game site, you always run the risk of flight delays. Once at the arrival airport, there can be rental-car issues. Hotels tend to be busy with other guests checking in between the five and seven p.m. window. So now you must wait patiently when all you want to do is get to your room and relax a few minutes before dinner and meetings start.

Such was the case for a particular game back in 2006. My crew was scheduled for an early game on Saturday morning in Gainesville, Florida. Kickoff was scheduled for high noon. We decided to complete all the pregame meetings on Friday evening.

The beginning of that workday for me was hectic, as some issues were behind schedule. I stayed until the very last minute and started driving south toward Florida around one p.m. My home was fifty miles north of Atlanta, which meant I had to deal with Friday traffic. Under normal conditions, I can make the drive to Gainesville in about five and a half hours.

Getting through Atlanta took a little longer than I had hoped. Once I got on the southside of the city, it was apparent that the earliest I could get to Gainesville would be seven o'clock. I would certainly miss dinner with the crew. I called ahead and gave our referee a heads-up that they shouldn't plan on me going with them to eat. I would meet them for our meeting after they returned to the hotel.

The drive from Atlanta takes you through Macon and into South Georgia. Some thirty miles north of Valdosta, Georgia, I ran into a late-September thunderstorm. The heavy rain combined with traffic slowed me down considerably. I had bad weather to Lake City, Florida.

I pulled into the hotel parking lot at almost eight p.m. The crew had already come back from dinner and was waiting on me in the meeting room. Instead of checking in, I grabbed my briefcase and went straight to pregame.

For the next three hours, we took a rules test, watched a conference-office-produced training video, and openly discussed our responsibilities of managing the game. The level of concentration required to navigate the meeting is intense.

At some point late in the meeting, we talked about how one particular team was prone to attempt a two-point conversion after they scored a touchdown. Specific conversation about what the center could and couldn't do prior to the snap was brought up. I contended that the rule book was clear that the center must be completely stationary before snapping the ball. I further explained that he couldn't be bent at the waist over the ball and reach down in one motion, throwing the ball to a teammate. He would need to place his hand on the ball, stop, and then proceed with starting the play. I was asked to provide the specific rule which stated this in the NCAA rule book. Everyone began looking in rule 7. Rule 7 covers snapping and passing the ball.

I'm cross-eyed at this point in the evening. It had been a long day and I hadn't had dinner. I stated, "Look under 7-4-2-b." That meant rule 7, section 4, article 2, and subsection b.

The rest of the crew is looking through their copy of the rule book. Finally, our referee blurts out, "There is no 7-4-2-b." When I realized that there wasn't, I simply said, "Well, there should be."

As a crew, we agreed that enough was enough. It was getting late, and it was time to go to our rooms. I had a pack of crackers and a coke for dinner.

IT SHOULDN'T HAVE TO BE THIS HARD

Ole Miss played at Arkansas on October 21, 2006. As it turns out, I probably should have skipped this game. Just kidding!

When I arrived at the Atlanta airport Friday for my flight to Fayetteville, Arkansas, I was informed that my flight had been canceled. Great! Delta had already confirmed me on a Continental Airlines flight. All I had to do was go to the gate and off I would go. So, off I went. When I arrived at the gate, the agent told me that the flight had already left an hour earlier. *What?*

Back I went to the Delta ticket counter in the main concourse. The line was long. While waiting to make my way to the front, I was simultaneously on hold, having called Delta's reservation customer service on the phone.

Two things had to happen: get on a flight, or drive all night to Fayetteville for an 11:30 a.m. central-time kickoff. There were six ticket agents at the end of this long line—five females and one male. The guy looked like a former player. I wanted that guy. Call me sexist if you want but I felt like maybe this guy would have sympathy for me. Some luck had swung in my favor. I got the guy!

"Sorry, sir, there are no other flights into Fayetteville this evening." That's when I dropped the "officiating card" on him. He replied, "Oh, cool. I've always wanted to do that."

He began typing on the keyboard in front of him. Each time he shook his head with displeasure. I finally told him that for me to make it driving, I would have to be leaving pretty soon.

Finally, he tells me, "I can get you as close as Little Rock."

"Book it, Danno!" I'll have a three-hour drive in front of me when we land.

I called Enterprise to rent a car. "Sorry, sir, we have no rental cars available." *Shit!*

I had a good friend who worked for Enterprise at the time. It was time to call in a favor. After explaining the situation to him, he tells me to sit tight and he'll call me back. I settled back in my seat on the plane train and proceeded to the concourse my flight is departing from.

Thirty minutes later, Chad calls me and tells me to ask for Cindy at the Enterprise rental counter when I get to Little Rock. She'll take care of me. For a while, things are moving along smoothly, but much later than originally scheduled.

The flight takes off from Atlanta and arrives in Little Rock as scheduled, eleven p.m. I got to the rental car area, and all the agencies appear closed, and there are no lights on. "Shit!" As I'm standing close to the Enterprise counter, this voice comes from behind the desk: "Are you Mr. Morris?"

Cindy had stayed two hours late just for me. She pointed me toward my rental car and I was off to Fayetteville just a few minutes after midnight.

I unlocked the door to my hotel room at 3:15 that Saturday morning. Whew, I could get a whole two hours and forty-five minutes of sleep before our 6:30 pregame meeting. I was sharing a room with the side judge that weekend. He was sound asleep.

Six o'clock came fast. I grabbed some oatmeal, a banana, and some yogurt from the continental breakfast and proceeded to our meeting room. It was time to shift into game mode.

After our pregame meeting, we dressed in our uniforms and left for the stadium at nine o'clock. The cool temperature helped me get fully awake.

Patrick Willis was the best player Ole Miss had on their team at the time. As a linebacker, he could move sideline to sideline as good as anyone playing football.

Right before the end of the first half, Arkansas ran a sweep to my side of the field. Willis, #52, had read the play perfectly. He grabbed the player by the waist to make the tackle. His momentum caused his feet to swing out behind his body. His left foot kicked me in my right thigh with the force of a sledgehammer. It took a couple of seconds for the pain to reach my brain. When it did, I went down like a rag doll. As the trainers were taking me to our locker room to assess my injury, the officials on the field made a few switches and completed the first half.

Nothing was broken but I did have a very deep bruise in the middle of my thigh. The trainers gave me plenty of ibuprofen, iced my leg, and suggested that they wrap my thigh with Ace bandages.

As the crew walked into the locker room for halftime, they saw me standing with my back facing them, uniform pants at my ankles. The trainer, innocently enough, was in front of me in a kneeling position, tightly wrapping my thigh. When *she* leaned out to the side of me from this position, I don't know who was more embarrassed, the crew or the trainer. I was good. I was able to finish the second half.

Since I was able to keep moving, the pain in my leg wasn't too bad. I was able to go to dinner with the crew. Doe's Eat Place was the restaurant we chose. Russ, Bobby, Greg, and I stayed at the table after everyone had eaten and gone back to the hotel. The owner knew us as officials and didn't mind us parking at one of his tables as we sat and drank beer.

I don't know whose idea it was, probably Greg's, but we ended up leaving with about six full plastic cups full of beer. It was an uphill walk back to the hotel. The beer buzz had numbed the pain in my leg. It was close to midnight, and I had to leave the hotel at 6:30 for my three-hour drive back to Little Rock the next morning. We all told each other "good night." Bobby and I headed up to our room. I asked him to make sure the alarm was set for six a.m. "Got it!"

I laid out my clothes on the floor by the bathroom so I could slip out of bed, take a quick shower, dress, and ease out of the room without disturbing Bobby. I think I was asleep before my head hit the pillow.

I killed the alarm within seconds of it going off. My leg screamed in pain when I tried to slip out of bed. I made it to the shower, packed, and limped to the lobby for a cup of coffee to begin my drive to Little Rock.

"What the hell? Why isn't the coffee ready?" There was no one in the lobby. I looked around for anybody. The night manager came out and asked me if I was checking in. "No, I was looking for a cup of coffee before I took off."

"Do you know what time it is?"

Just then I noticed the clock above the desk—three a.m.! "Shit!" Do I sleep in the lobby or go to my room? I had left my key on the dresser when I left a few minutes earlier. With pain in my leg, I made the decision that if Gus was up, Bobby should get up.

I knocked on the door long enough for Bobby to wake up and let me in.

"Do you remember what time you set the clock for?"

"Yes, six o'clock."

"Wrong, genius!"

I was able to sleep in my clothes for two hours. For the next six hours, as I began my journey home, my leg was immobile. Every hour that passed caused it to tighten up even more. The three-hour car ride back to Little Rock was uneventful. The flight back to Atlanta was on time and very smooth. The wait for the shuttle bus to take me to my car was very short. By the time I got home, I was in agony. I had a huge knot in my thigh. After a few beers, I was able to cut the grass and get a few chores done before the start of a new week.

People tell me all the time about how great it must be to travel around and officiate football. Yeah, it's really great! Particularly when your flight gets canceled.

DON'T BREAK
FROM ROUTINE

In December of 2011, I was assigned to work the Beef O'Brady Bowl at Tropicana Field in St. Petersburg, Florida. Having blown a call during the last play of my last regular season game during the Vanderbilt at Tennessee game, I didn't deserve to be at this bowl game. However, Steve Shaw, the coordinator of SEC football officials, told me that he wanted me in that game for no other reason than he didn't want my season to end on that bad of a note.

The Beef O'Brady Bowl was one of the lower tier games. Being played on December 20, it was one of the first bowls of the season to be played.

On the prior Sunday evening, I had hosted a very casual Christmas open house. It didn't run too late in the evening, as I was going to fly to Tampa the next morning for this game.

While getting ready for my open house, I cleaned up the garage, leaving plenty of room for my car. I always parked in the driveway, but I figured with people coming over, I would leave extra room for their vehicles.

I followed the same routine for years when it came to packing my gear for weekend football trips. Immediately after washing it when I got home from my most recent game, I would repack my bag, following the sequence that I would put things on. The afternoon of or evening before I was to leave for my next game, I would take everything out and repack one more time, just to make sure I didn't forget anything. After this was done, I would put everything by the front door, ready to go in the car when I left for my trip.

Following this routine, I never forgot anything during my career. That was until December of 2011.

Being that I had parked my car in the garage, I walked out through the door leading there. I had checked all the lights in the house, turned on the alarm, and locked the door behind me. It was about 5:15 in the morning. I had scheduled a morning flight to Tampa, Florida.

I had left the house in plenty of time. I had a fresh cup of coffee and began my drive to the Atlanta airport. I had the right music on the radio, it was close to Christmas, and I was thinking back on how nice the open house had gone the night before. As I drove, I thought how lucky I was to be able to work the assignment I was traveling to.

Three quarters of the way through my fifty-mile drive to the airport, panic set in. I reached over the back of my seat and sure enough, my bag and backpack were not in the car. They were right where I had left them for the previous four years. I moved into this house in 2007. This particular morning was one of the first times I had left the house through the garage door. *Now what the hell am I going to do?* I couldn't call anyone at that early hour. And if I did, how would they get into the house to get my stuff without setting off the alarm? Where would I meet them? There were too many complications. The only recourse I had was to return home.

During my return drive home, I called Southwest Airlines and explained the situation. There were still seats on a later flight, but I needed to hurry. I turned around at the Cascade Road/I-285 exit and began driving frantically back toward my house. Relaxation had been replaced by high anxiety. How could I have been so careless?

I pulled into the driveway, unlocked the front door, and grabbed my gear. Back to the airport I went. I usually park offsite, and I did so on this trip. All the way to the airport, I was hoping there would still be seats. If not, I would have to drive to Tampa for the following day's game.

My first stop was at the Southwest ticket counter. I told the lady helping me what happened. She began to type on her keyboard and said, "You might still make this flight, but you've got to go now!"

I replied, "Just put me on the next flight, I'm tired of being in a hurry. It's no problem."

My flight landed about an hour and forty-five minutes after the one I was supposed to be on. It turned out that it really wasn't a problem. My first obligation in St. Petersburg was to attend the team luncheon. I made that with a few minutes to spare. Afterward, I went and checked into the host hotel. I decided I would walk across the street and get a haircut. When I returned, I ran into Hubert Owens. He also lived in Atlanta and would be the referee on the crew.

He invited me up to his room and he shared a couple of Stella Artois beers. Finally, some routine had been reestablished. The game was pretty uneventful.

NO, I'M NOT
GOING TO CALL THAT

Jackie Sherrill was a hard-nose, old-school football coach. He was stern, but fair. Sherrill helped Coach Bear Bryant win two national championships in the mid-sixties at Alabama. Working his sideline was always an experience. While he was at Mississippi State, he had one particularly good year, from a winning perspective. He won several games where his team had to come back from being behind to win. One such game was at Auburn.

I drove down the morning of the game in plenty of time to have lunch and begin getting ready for our midafternoon kickoff. I was reminded during the pregame meeting that we want to do as much preventive officiating as possible. Basically, what this means is that we are going to talk to players when they begin to do things that might create a problem later in the game. It holds the number of penalties to a minimum but, more importantly, it changes the players behavior.

Early in the game, Auburn attempted a field goal and made it. The formation could have been a little better with the tackles not bowed back so much. After the play, I ran onto the field and talked with the players about getting up onto the line of scrimmage. The line judge, on the other side of the field, also spoke with the coaches and told them to get their players to line up properly.

The next time Auburn attempted a field goal, the formation was better but still not up to Coach Sherrill's liking.

As I'm in position waiting on the ball to be snapped, Coach Sherrill, as he was prone to do, is standing directly behind me yelling, "They're not legal!" When he starts this kind of shit, if it's not absolutely illegal, I'm damn sure not going to call it.

After the score, we go into a TV time out. Jackie walked right out in front of me and asked me, "Are you going to call *that* illegal formation?" referring to the previous play. I simply replied, "No." Coach Sherrill said, "Okay," and walked off.

Monday afternoon, I get a phone call from Bobby Gaston, the SEC coordinator of football officials. The call went something like this:

Bobby: "Good afternoon, Gus, it's Bobby. How are you?"

Me: "I'm good, how about you?"

Bobby: "Gus, Coach Sherrill said you told him you were not going to call illegal formation."

Me: "No, that's not what I told him. I said I was not going to call illegal formation on that one particular play. We had talked with the Auburn players, and they had moved up closer to the line of scrimmage."

Bobby: "Okay, how's your mom and dad?"

Me: "Everybody's good."

Bobby: "All right, I'll call Jackie back. See you around the campus."

That was the end of that.

During another game in Starkville, Mississippi, I was on the opposite sideline of Coach Sherrill and had a good view from across the field.

The center for the opposing team tended to have his head slightly beyond the ball when snapping for punts. Is this technically a foul? Maybe. Would we ever call it? Hell no!

So, the first time the visiting team must punt, Coach Sherrill starts losing his mind. He is standing directly behind Mike Shirey, the line judge. Arms flailing, he's yelling in Mike's ear that the center is offsides. "He's offsides! He's offsides! He's offsides!" he's screaming repeatedly with the pitch of his voice getting higher as he's ranting. At first, Mike has a look of irritation on his face. But then he almost laughs because it is just so comical. I had a free view of the entire performance.

Word is, Coach Sherrill has a collection of clowns. Seriously!

FAN-HURLING CHAMPIONSHIPS

Transporting the SEC officials to and from the stadium is taken very seriously. Generally, the crowds around the venues are enjoying the atmosphere of game day and having a great time. Still, you must be careful and prepared for what could happen.

The officials leave the hotel for the stadium, fully dressed in uniform, around two and a half hours prior to the scheduled kickoff time. This can vary depending on the distance to the stadium and anticipated traffic in the area. We were encouraged to travel light and fast. Get in the van, no talking, all business.

The van driver is usually the same person, week after week, year after year. In some instances, the chain crews meet up at the hotels and everyone goes together. The caravan is escorted under police protection from the time we leave the hotel until we reach the stadium. LSU and South Carolina personnel provide the most intense rolling roadblocks through traffic. There is no mistake on what is happening as the officials make their approach. The drop-off point is inside the secure gates, close to our designated room.

Mississippi State's van driver is a legend when it comes to this position. Everett Kennard was the transportation manager for the university. He drove teams everywhere. He knows where all the skeletons are buried.

Shortly after leaving the Holiday Inn Express in Starkville to journey over to Davis-Wade Stadium, he goes into his well-rehearsed diatribe about crazy fan behavior—getting your ass in the van immediately after the game, etc. First-year officials sometimes question their sanity of officiating when they hear Everett explain what *could* happen.

One particular weekend in Starkville, I had been assigned as an alternate official for the Arkansas versus Mississippi State game. It was a miserable day weather-wise. It was overcast and cold. When it was all said and done, we experienced rain, sleet, and snow with some minor accumulation. As an AO, you don't get to move around much to help stay warm. My hands and feet were numb. Plus, the game went into overtime. Life, at that moment, was miserable.

As soon as the game was over, we hightailed it to the van. Everett was there with the van warmed up and doors open. It takes a couple of minutes for the referee to remove the stadium microphone system and return it to the individual responsible for its safe keeping until the next game.

Arkansas prevailed that afternoon in what was a very competitive game. Saying the Mississippi State fans were not happy would be an understatement. Everett never let being a Mississippi State employee effect the way he performed his duties in transporting the officials.

There were a couple of State fans near the van who were berating us unmercifully. We were threatened and called about every name in the book. Most of the time, this is harmless.

One guy kept moving closer to us. Everett first told him to get back. It escalated quickly, so he yelled at the fan to move away. I think alcohol had impaired the fan's ability to hear. When he got closer than he should have, Everett grabbed him by the back of the collar and belt, spun him around, and hurled him liked a Frisbee. It was a feat of beauty. After flying through the air, the fan landed square on his ass. Not really sure what just happened, he began to start running his mouth again. Everett took one step toward him, and the words miraculously and instantaneously ceased.

The officials gave Everett a 9.8. The alternate gave him a perfect 10.

BAD BODY LANGUAGE ENDED WITH GOOD RESULTS

In late September of 2005, I was assigned to work as the alternate official in the Wyoming versus Ole Miss game in Oxford, Mississippi. The Cowboys beat the Rebels, 24–14.

Ole Miss was not playing well. There was a lot of poor execution and bad timing. Frustration showed in their coaches, players, and fans. As the AO, I moved up and down the home-team sideline while operating the game clock.

At some point in the fourth quarter, there was a personal foul called by an on-field official directly in front of me. It was a good call, no question about it. Even the player knew he had committed the foul. As the penalty is being marked off, someone behind me starts berating the officials. He's questioning the enforcement and stating, unequivocally, that the officials are wrong. Without turning around, I just shake my head from side to side in disagreement with this guy. Well, he noticed me, and things started downhill in a hurry. He's saying, "You don't have any idea who I am," "You won't ever work here again." *Blah, blah, blah.*

For some reason, we went into a TV time out right after the enforcement. Somebody may have called a team time out, or we may have had a player injury. And this guy was still on my ass. Then, he threatened me. The line was crossed.

I handed off the clock switch to the person that helps me with the cord while moving up and down the sideline. "I'll be right back."

I walked up to this guy, who is standing with two of his buddies. "What's your name?" He went silent. His buddies took a step back and went silent. There was a Mississippi state trooper standing nearby. I told him to "Keep him away from me." There were no problems during the rest of the game.

When we got back to the hotel, our replay official wanted to know what I was dealing with on the sideline. They had seen it all from the booth. I told him what had happened.

"Do you know who he was?"

"No, I have no idea."

Replay insisted that we report the incident to the Southeastern Conference office. I told Mike he can report it if he wants to; I didn't see the need.

While the crew was going through the postgame debriefing, I started looking through the game program to see if I could figure out who was giving me such a hard time. Picture by picture, page by page, I searched. Suddenly, that's him, clear as day. Danny Nutt, the Ole Miss head coach's brother. Well, that's great. At the time, no, I had no idea who he was, but I did then. I didn't hear anything about the incident over the next week.

The following Saturday, October 1, my regular crew was in Knoxville for our game between Tennessee and Ole Miss. During warm-ups, I spotted Danny Nutt on the field. I was talking with our back judge when I realized who it was. I told him, "I'll be right back."

I walked over to Danny and the first thing he did was sincerely apologize for what had happened the previous weekend. We shook hands and I told him that I wanted this to be behind us and for us to move on. He agreed and everything was over.

The following summer, I worked a preseason scrimmage at Ole Miss. My daughter, Susan, was enrolled there. She was at the scrimmage with me and hung out around the field before and during the practice. While the two of us were standing together talking, Danny Nutt walked over to say "Hello." Everything was good. I introduced Susan to him and let him know that she was a student at Ole Miss. Danny immediately reached into his wallet and pulled out a business card. He handed it to Susan. "This is my cell phone number. If you ever need anything, do not hesitate to call me."

My improper body language, along with Danny's inappropriate behavior, started things off in the wrong direction. But two people who understand the importance of football, were able to bring things back to where they should be. It made me feel very comfortable that there was another person at Ole Miss that would help my daughter. Oh, Tennessee beat Ole Miss, 27–10.

DON'T TELL HIM I SAID THAT TO YOU

Troy State played Georgia in Athens one afternoon. Troy had a pretty good team, but they were no match for the Bulldogs. Larry Blakeney was the successful head coach for the Trojans. Out of frustration during the second half, Blakeney jumped my shit.

We were working a good game and I knew things had gotten to him. Nothing that he said was personal. When he finished unloading on me, I turned to him and told him that Bill Junkin wanted me to tell him "Hello!" Bill was a customer of mine and a first cousin of Larry.

Coach Blakeney put his hand on my shoulder, smiled, and said, "Please don't tell him what I said to you!"

NO, I'M DEFINITELY NOT ON HIS CHRISTMAS CARD LIST

The date of October 11, 1997, was very close to being the beginning of the end for my officiating career in the Southeastern Conference. The incident that caused all the hubbub occurred during the Florida versus LSU game in Baton Rouge, Louisiana. At the time of the game, Florida was ranked number one in the nation. LSU stood at number fourteen.

I took half a day off from work on Thursday, October 9, and a full day off on the tenth in order to drive to Baton Rouge with my girlfriend, Cheryl. The cost to fly that week-end was more than I wanted to pay. The Florida fans had booked most of the flights and the remaining tickets were very expensive.

We left Alpharetta, Georgia, around noon on that Thursday and drove to Biloxi, Mississippi, to spend the night. We had dinner at a local seafood restaurant and got back to our hotel before it got too late. The next morning, while Cheryl was getting ready, I walked across the street and bought two large cups of coffee. It was a little specialty shop, and the coffee was really good. Really strong too.

The remaining drive to Baton Rouge was only two hours and fifteen minutes. We timed our trip to arrive in Baton Rouge in time for lunch. We were able to get an early check-in. The car was unloaded, and we put our luggage in the room. We had a quiet, ground-floor room that opened up to

41

the courtyard of the hotel. I called the front desk to see if any other crew members had check in yet, in case they wanted to join us for lunch. We were the first to arrive.

Since we were the only ones among the crew, we drove across to the other side of the highway and had lunch at TJ Ribs. The Friday-afternoon lunch crowd was busier than usual because of the game that was being played at LSU the next evening.

After loading up on barbeque and sweet tea, we headed back to the hotel. A nap was in order after all we had eaten. The rooms at the hotel were very comfortable. The best part, to me, were the black-out curtains. Once closed, the room was dark—even in the middle of the day. We slept for a couple of hours.

When we woke up and gathered our senses, I saw that I had a message waiting for me from the front desk. Doyle Jackson had left word for me to call him in his room. Since his room was a couple of doors down the hall, I walked down and knocked on his door. We spoke for a few minutes about the agenda for the following day. He also told me he was going to stay in for dinner that night, for us to go on and have dinner without him.

With the schedule set, Cheryl and I decided to have dinner by ourselves. It seemed each crew member had their own idea about what they wanted to eat. I called a place named Juban's, pulled a few strings, and got a reservation for two. This restaurant is just around the corner from the hotel. It is really nice. The Redfish Adrian with a wedge salad is by far the best entrée in Baton Rouge.

Saturday morning started with breakfast in the small hotel lobby. Our pregame meeting was scheduled for nine a.m. That would provide plenty of time during the day to watch other games around the conference before we left to make our way to Tiger Stadium. The amount of waiting during the day of a night game can be taxing. This weekend was a little different.

The weather was pleasant and having a room that opened up to the courtyard made things much easier to tolerate.

We opened up our room to have access to the courtyard. Cheryl spent most of the day by the pool reading books. I went back and forth, talking with her and watching football in our room. The temperature was in the upper eighties during the day.

Because kickoff was at six p.m. central time, we had to leave for the stadium no later than 3:45. Cheryl was able to ride to and from the stadium with one of the deputies that escorted our caravan. The only bad part about this required her to leave her seat and be back in his patrol car before the game was over. If she's not there in time, we would have to leave without her.

One other issue she had to contend with was entertaining herself due to arriving at the stadium so early before kickoff. She wandered through the tailgaters and made new friends among the fans outside the stadium.

This game was in ESPN's prime-time slot on that Saturday evening. Tiger Stadium was packed, and the weather was perfect. It was a great night for college football.

Florida won the coin toss and deferred their option to the second half. LSU then elected to receive the kickoff. On LSU's first possession, they drove down the field to the Florida twenty-two-yard line and fumbled the ball, giving it to the Gators.

At the end of the first quarter, the score was 14–7 in favor of the Tigers. After a scoreless second quarter by both teams, we went into halftime with LSU leading by seven points. The Tiger faithful were very much into the game. The crowd noise was very loud.

Florida was set to receive the opening kickoff of the second half. On their first possession of the third quarter, the offense came to life, and they scored quickly. It took the Gators a mere two minutes and forty-three seconds to put the ball in the endzone. Florida had tied the game, 14 all. Neither team scored during the remainder of the third quarter.

On the very first play of the fourth quarter, Florida had to punt. LSU's offense went four plays and out, punting the ball back to Florida with 13:30 remaining in the game. The kick went into the endzone, resulting in a touchback for the Gators.

On Florida's second play of the series, Doug Johnson, the Gators' quarterback, threw an interception that was picked off by Cedric Donaldson and returned for an LSU touchdown. After the successful extra point, LSU had retaken the lead, 21–14. Tiger Stadium was going crazy.

LSU kicked off to Florida with thirteen minutes on the clock. During the return, the ball was fumbled by Bo Carroll, of Florida, and recovered by LSU on the Gator thirty-yard line. Four plays later, Herb Tyler walked in for an LSU touchdown. The successful extra point made the score 28–14, in favor of LSU. The Tigers had scored two touchdowns off of Florida turnovers in the course of one minute and thirty-three seconds.

With the ability of the Florida offense, there was still plenty of time on the game clock to get back into the game. Florida scored on their next possession with 6:40 remaining. They had cut the lead to seven. The atmosphere from the stands in Tiger Stadium had changed. Nervousness was setting in.

The following LSU possession resulted in no points being scored. They were, however, able to keep good field position. After punting the ball back to Florida, the Gators had to start on their own twenty-one-yard line. The clock showed 4:20 when Florida took back over on offense. There still plenty of time, considering their capacity for scoring. Florida ran a couple of plays and ended up with third down and eight yards to go on their twenty-two-and-a-half-yard line with 3:20 left. Florida's quarterback, Doug Johnson, had gotten hit hard and was replaced by Jesse Palmer. The crowd noise in the stadium had increased due to the LSU fans' reaction to this change on offense. It was extremely loud.

Just prior to the ball being snapped to start the third-down play, a Florida wide receiver moved early. I immediately had a flag down for a false start, killing the play. Anything else that occurred during the play was irrelevant. Because the players and other officials couldn't hear my whistle, the play continued. Palmer had thrown the ball down field, and it was caught for what appeared to be a first down. Once I reached our referee, I reported that I had a false start against the offense. We took the ball back to the previous spot, stepped off five yards, and set up for the next play. It would now be third and thirteen from the Gator seventeen-and-a-half-yard line.

When I turned toward the sideline to move the down box to the correct yard line, I found myself face to face with Coach Spurrier. We were around the bottom of the numbers, a place where he wasn't supposed to be. With very animated body language, he screamed at me, with what sounded like, "You're full of shit!" Without hesitation, I penalized him for unsportsmanlike conduct. Rumor has it that this was the only unsportsmanlike foul he ever got over the course of his career. As soon as my flag hit the ground, the volume in Tiger Stadium went way up. The crowd could clearly see that Coach Spurrier had been penalized.

I turned back to Doyle and reported the foul. Doyle's response: "Okey dokey." By rule, this is a fifteen-yard penalty. However, because the ball was sitting on the seventeen-and-a-half yard line, the penalty took the ball half the distance to the goal line. It was now Florida's ball, third and twenty-two from just inside the nine-yard line.

Prior to the next play, Doug Johnson came back into the ballgame. From a technical standpoint, the clock showed 3:18 remaining in the game. Because the false start was a dead ball foul and the game clock was not going to start until the snap, we should have reset the game clock to 3:20. On third down, Johnson threw another interception. LSU took over and ran out the clock.

When the clock hit zero, we were on the south end of the field. The way we had to leave the field was on the north end of the field. As we turned to run in that direction, we met students that were rushing the field around the fifty-yard line. It was a scary feeling. There were hundreds of fans on the field for every one official.

We eventually made our way to the tunnel, through the equipment room area of the LSU locker room, and finally outside the stadium where the vans were waiting on us. There was absolutely no one outside the stadium. It was a really weird situation. In no time, we had all loaded up and the police-escorted caravan began making our way back to the hotel. Just before I stepped into the official's van, I looked toward one of the lead vehicles and yes, Cheryl had gotten to the car prior to us leaving. One less thing to worry about.

Due to the fact that there was no traffic, we made it back to the hotel in no time at all. We decided to go ahead and do our postgame meeting before showering. Eddie Powers and Gerald Hodges offered their room for us to meet in. The TV was on a local channel, and they were broadcasting live from Tiger Stadium. The field was still completely covered with LSU faithful. Most of the camera angles were from the press box, above the field. Fans were celebrating and a few were looking for keepsakes of this huge upset. LSU had defeated the number-one ranked Florida Gators.

We noticed a group of guys in the crowd carrying out the down marker and line-to-gain equipment. That'll look good in the fraternity house. As we sat watching the scene playing out on TV, it became apparent that the ripped down goal-posts posed difficulties for the fans in taking them out through the tunnels underneath the stadium. Realizing that they couldn't get them out that way, the large group started carrying the goalposts up the steps of the stadium. A "herd mentality" had developed, and apparently, they decided that the only way to get their prize out of the stadium was to throw it over the top. Enough cops showed up and stopped this potential disaster. The goalposts were returned to the field, disassembled, and taken out piece by piece. We turned the TV off and went through the short postgame meeting.

It was late when we wrapped up our meeting and game reports. I was starving; we had to get something to eat. Ted Davis, our umpire, told me he knew a place where we could go. "You and Cheryl ride with me and we'll go there." We went into the bar/restaurant, and it immediately became clear that there was no real food available. There were some nuts and chips, but that was it. We had a couple of drinks while Ted did his thing around the bar. Finally, it got to the point early in the morning where we really needed to get back to the hotel. I don't know exactly what Ted had gotten into, but he was absolutely in no shape to drive. In fact, I had to help him walk to his rental car. Besides being hungry, I was frustrated with having to take care of Ted. I managed to get him in the back seat, and he went straight to sleep. I drove back to the hotel while Cheryl rode shotgun. It's about two o'clock in the morning, at this point.

Getting Ted into his room was a major undertaking. He was hard to wake up in the car and couldn't walk under his own power. We made our way into the hotel and to the door of his room. I wedged myself against him, propping him up against the wall in the hallway. I then rummaged through his pocket until I found his room key. Once I got him in the room, I laid him on the bed and took off his shoes. I put the car keys and room card on the bedside table, turned off the lights, closed the door behind me. Now it was our turn to go to bed.

The next morning, the phone rang and woke us up. When

I answered it, all I heard was, "Where's the car?" No good morning or anything. I told Ted where I had parked it when we came in earlier that morning. "Okay, I'll see you in a couple of weeks." We were off the following week.

Cheryl and I had overslept. The room was so dark and quiet that we didn't get up as early as we had planned. We had a long drive back home so we hurried and got on the road as quickly as we could. We arrived back home around 8:30 that evening.

At some point during the drive, my dad called and wanted a play-by-play of the situation with Coach Spurrier. I told him what all had happened. "Good," he replied. There was not a lot of love lost between Georgia Tech people and Coach Spurrier.

The following Monday morning started off like most others—pretty normal. Around 9:30 in the morning, I was paged at work for a phone call. When I picked it up, Bobby Gaston was on the other end of the call. He was the coordinator of football officials. He asked me to give him the details of what had happened with Coach Spurrier during the game in Baton Rouge. I gave my side of the story. He said, "Thank you," and we ended the call. I'm thinking everything is okay.

Around 10:30, I get another page for a phone call. This time, when I answer it, Commissioner Roy Kramer is on the other end of the call. This phone call was a little more contentious. Kramer started implying that I had determined the outcome of the game and that my call was incorrect.

"If you look at the play, frame by frame, it doesn't look like a false start."

"Commissioner, I don't have the benefit of officiating a play frame by frame," I replied. We talked for a few more minutes when he handed the phone to Bobby. Bobby told me he would call me later at home.

This was not good.

Over the next several days, I began to receive phone calls of support from fellow officials. I was being threatened with termination as an official from the league office. Other members of the association were fully in support of me and plans to retaliate against the conference were being put together if I was fired. The media had picked it up. Most were in favor of what I had done. Some favored Spurrier. The athletic director at Florida had even gotten into the mix, apparently demanding that the SEC get rid of me.

On Thursday evening, I called Bobby Gaston and told him something had to happen. This situation was causing too much distraction. I had gotten a letter from Commissioner Kramer on SEC letterhead informing me that I was essentially on "Double Secret" probation. That officials should not be determining the outcome of games. Bobby asked me what I thought should happen, and I offered a possible solution.

"Bobby, I'm scheduled to be off this weekend. Why don't you put out a statement that the official involved in the Florida-LSU game will not be working this weekend." All of this was true. It might calm the waters. Bobby agreed that this was a good idea and released the statement. Over the course of a few weeks, things returned to normal.

I survived this political storm and a few others later on in my career. Sure, coaches would get upset with a call, but few held a grudge, like Coach Spurrier. My father used to remind me that, "This, too, shall pass." With Spurrier, it didn't and hasn't to this day. There were a total of 102 SEC head coaches during my thirty-one years working with the league. Spurrier was just one of them. Still, I'm not on his Christmas-card list.

WHAT'S THAT SOUND?

In my early years as an official, the Acme Thunderer was the Cadillac of whistles. I used two whistles during my games. Both were attached to lanyards, one around my neck and the other around my left wrist. The wrist lanyard made it easy to let go of the whistle and freed up both hands to handle a football.

In 1987, Ron Foxcroft and Charles Sheppard introduced their Fox40 whistle during the Pan American Games. This was a "pea-less" design. In 1998, they received a patent for their effort. It became the most used whistle in all of sports.

The SEC coordinator of officials supplied every official with this new design. It even came with the SEC logo. I've got roughly twenty-five hanging around in my closet. I continued to use my Acme Thunderer. It was a chrome-plated, brass whistle with a little cork ball inside. That was the pea. You had to place a rubber guard on the end where you blew into. If not, it was not uncommon for a tooth to chip when in use.

For years, people questioned why I wasn't using the Fox40. Steve Shaw persisted the most at trying to get me to change. Anyone on his crew should be using the latest and greatest.

"The Thunderer is tried and true. Why change what works?" Switching out would have been "change." I was a rebel.

Our crew was selected to work the 2007 SEC Championship game. It's a tremendous honor to be selected to officiate this game. The weekend in Atlanta is far and away better than any bowl assignment. Except maybe a national championship. I'll never know.

After dressing in our uniforms, we congregated in the hospitality suite of the Hyatt on Peachtree Street. As a crew, we went down the elevators and into the awaiting vans to take us to the stadium. No one noticed.

For two-plus hours, we milled around the small dressing room, talking, watching other championship games, and eating pregame snacks. It seems like an eternity but the anticipation of getting the game started eases any anxiety.

Finally, it's time for kickoff. About two plays into the game, I have a play run to my sideline and the runner is tackled after a short two yards. When I blow my whistle to indicate the ball is dead, Steve Shaw's eyes open wide, and a smile comes over his face. I had accepted change and switched over to the Fox40. I had resisted for as long as I could.

A few years later, I had the pleasure of introducing myself to Ron Foxcroft. He said he knew who I was.

"Really?" I asked.

"Yep, Steve Shaw told me about you during y'all's championship game!"

My Acme Thunderer is still around and has an eternal resting place among my officiating memorabilia.

BIG BASS DRUM

I had two weird things happen to me while working games at Auburn that were not football related. Sometime in the middle '90s, I was working a night game in Jordan-Hare Stadium. Right as I took my first step during the opening kickoff, I bug flew into my left ear.

It wasn't a big bug. Tried as I did, I couldn't reach in far enough with my finger to coax it out. It wasn't painful but it was incredibly aggravating. I could feel it crawling around, searching for a way out. It kept going in the wrong direction.

Occasionally, it found its way onto my ear drum. While walking around on that part of my ear, it begins playing out of rhythm with the Band.

Finally, halftime arrived. A trainer from Auburn came into our locker room. He flushed out my ear. I don't know how he found one but when the gnat was finally removed from my ear, it was wearing a tiny Auburn marching band uniform.

The other weird thing happened in the locker room well before the game. The Auburn athletic staff places water, sports drinks, light food, and snacks in the room for the officials. I spotted something new to me and thought I would give it a try.

There are these gummy things that are supposed to provide added energy. They come in various flavors. The cherry-flavored ones caught my attention. I unwrapped it and popped in my mouth. They are soft and incredibly sticky. I didn't really know if you should just kind of suck on them or chew, but chew is what I did.

After about my third bite, excruciating pain pierced through my upper jaw. A crown had come loose and the nerve under it let me know that it was not excited about being exposed to any type of air. Matter of fact, it wasn't excited about being exposed to anything.

Fortunately, I was able to save the crown. I placed it in one of my front pockets in hopes that it could be salvaged by my dentist when I got home.

I worked the entire game while trying to figure out how to minimize the pain in my mouth. One thing that I could not learn to do effectively was to blow a whistle without almost being brought to my knees. Short blasts were about all I could muster. Some plays ended without a whistle at all.

And yes, my dentist was able to salvage the crown. Under warranty, at that.

SOCIAL MEDIA MESSAGE BOARDS

Some officials live and breathe by what is written about them in blogs and on message boards. It doesn't change anything, and it shouldn't influence how you go about doing your job.

I've explained to newer officials that they should stay away from those types of social media outlets. My reasoning? The coaches hardly know the rules, how can you expect the average fan to know them? Plus, they have the added advantage of seeing replays dozens of times, from multiple angles and in slow motion.

I believe it was Morgan Freeman who said, "Don't take criticism from someone you wouldn't seek advice from." It's a good approach for an official to take when dealing with social media.

Officials are completely abused in social media. There's no accountability for people or groups that make incorrect statements. They may have passion, but they suffer no consequences for their actions. Unfortunately, it's impossible for information to be corrected before things spiral out of control.

Sometimes, subtle threats are made against officials. As an active SEC official, we were reminded that if we received a threat, we were to report it to the conference office. My question was, *What, if anything, can they do for me when I live almost two hundred miles away from Birmingham?* I guess the optics of saying something like that helped the overall image of the conference. I just hoped no one was foolish enough to come over to my house and try to cause harm. I've got a very clear, unobstructed view all the way around my house. And I can make it difficult to navigate.

On October 19, 2019, I was in Columbia, South Carolina. The Gators and the Gamecocks kicked off at noon on that Saturday. Through three quarters, it was a really good game. They were tied 10 all at the half. South Carolina led, 20–17, at the end of the third quarter. Then Florida really came alive and outscored South Carolina, 21–7, in the fourth quarter. The final score favored the Gators, 38–27.

During Florida's last scoring drive, we missed an offensive pass-interference foul. Bad. There was a crossing route that started from the right side of the formation. I took my eyes off the initial receiver I was responsible for. I was hoping the back judge would pick up this guy while I turned my attention to another receiver that was in my area. By the time the back judge picked him up, it was too late. An illegal pick sprung another receiver, he caught the pass and scored a touchdown, untouched.

The touchdown occurred right in front of the student section. They were not happy with our missed call. They had a clear view of it and there is no denying we didn't.

I returned home the next day around 12:30 p.m. After I said "Hello" to my dog, I unpacked my uniform and threw it in the washing machine. I grabbed a beer from the refrigerator and sat out on my front porch. Not long after, I got a text from an unknown number threatening physical harm against me because of the missed call the day before. I went and got another beer from the refrigerator.

As it turned out, somehow, some of the crew's personal information had been "doxed" to the public through a certain message board. Who did it? We never found out. If the Southeastern Conference office knew who it was, they never let us know. At least they didn't let me know.

I never felt seriously threatened but understood the seriousness it could bring. Unfortunately, someday, someone is going to carry through with a threat. Unless someone holds a grudge against me, like Coach Spurrier does, I probably won't have to deal with any more acts of intimidation due to my officiating.

I'M GOING TO GET YOUR JOB

My fourth SEC Championship game was in December of 2008. This was a matchup between the University of Alabama and the University of Florida. Alabama finished the regular season with a number-one ranking in the country in numerous polls. Florida was ranked number one in the AP poll. It was going to be a very big game.

The game met all the expectations of the hype leading up to it. Florida led, 17–10, at halftime, and Alabama led, 20–17, at the end of the third quarter. In the fourth quarter, Florida, led by Tim Tebow, took control of the game, and scored two touchdowns, winning by a final score of 31–20.

The game had been officiated well. Our referee didn't have to announce too many penalties. Both teams played with discipline, with national championship implications at stake for each of them.

On Florida's last drive of the game, things changed. On four plays prior to their final touchdown, Urban Meyer left the coaches area and walked down to the twelve-yard line to call plays into the offensive huddle. I was working on the Florida sideline; therefore, it was my responsibility to move him back to the team area, which I did. I also reminded him, and his "Get Back" coach, that he couldn't come down the sideline that far.

Two plays later, he's right back where I ran him off before, except now to the eleven-yard line. He had been very clearly warned the previous time I took him back to the sideline. This time, I dropped my penalty marker for committing an unsportsmanlike conduct foul. Florida was inside the Alabama ten-yard line, and this backed them up fifteen yards. Leading Alabama by only four points, this was a big foul. Two plays later, Florida scores their last touchdown, making the margin of victory eleven points.

During the touchdown and the succeeding kickoff, we go into our last commercial break. Florida's kicking team is getting organized on their sideline. I look up field and Urban Meyer is pointing at me and yelling in my direction. I decided to move toward him so I could hear what he was saying.

He's really showing his anger when I get close to him. Finally, before walking away, he says something to me that sounded like, "I'm going to get your job!" Who knows? It was so loud in the stadium it was hard to hear anything clearly. Anyway, *he* walked away first, not me. I'm thinking to myself, *Which one?*

I was pissed. This didn't need to happen, but it did. The crew was 100 percent behind my call. When we got back to the hotel after the game, my emotions were running a little high. The coordinator of officials acted as if what happened at the end of the game wasn't a big deal.

It had been a point of emphasis to keep the coaches off the field during games. I took pride in being able to manage my sidelines. Prior to this game getting started, I spoke with Coach Meyer about staying off the field. He agreed that he would. Instead of penalizing him the first time, I decided to warn him without threatening what would happen if he did it again. Apparently, he didn't take me seriously.

The following Monday, I called the SEC office and left word asking our coordinator of officials to give me a call. He finally called me back the following Thursday afternoon. During our conversation, he ended up reading me a letter that he had received from Coach Meyer. The letter indicated that the unsportsmanlike call I made during the game should not be made in that type of environment. Our coordinator didn't come right out and say it, but I felt like he agreed with the coach.

Toward the end of the call, he told me something like, "But the conference is going to back you up on this." It was at that point that I didn't feel like we had the full support of our leader. My schedule for the next several years, which is put together by the coordinator and signed off on by the commissioner, was an embarrassment. I felt like I was back on the "Homecoming Tour."

Later on that Thursday afternoon, my cell phone rang, showing an unrecognizable number. When I answered, the person identified himself by saying, "Gus, this is Willie." Willie had been a defensive assistant coach for years around the league. I first got to know him when he was the defensive coordinator at the University of Georgia. He can hit a golf ball as far as anyone.

He told me the reason that he called was for me to know that he and many other coaches around the league were very pleased with my penalty on Coach Meyer. "You're one of only a few officials that has the guts to penalize him." I told him how this should not have happened, that I didn't go out there looking for it. "You did what you had to do. He left you no choice."

We talked for a few more minutes. I thanked him for calling me and that it was good to hear from him. Don't be a stranger.

After we ended the call, I realized that it was much more important to have the respect of my peers than for me to have certain expectations from the conference office. I can damn sure live with that.

NOBODY CALLS MY REFEREE A LIAR

For some reason, Fayetteville, Arkansas, provided more weird and unusual situations than any other game site. I also was assigned four or more Tulsa at Arkansas games over the course of my career.

On September 6, 2003, I had one such game. Tulsa and Arkansas are geographically close to one another. They've had some pretty good games over the years, but Arkansas has dominated the series with fifty-five wins compared to fifteen wins for the Golden Hurricane. This game was won handily by the Razorbacks, 45–13.

I flew directly into the Northwest Arkansas Regional Airport on the previous afternoon. Two of my crewmates, Rocky Goode and Gerald Hodges, had landed a little earlier and were waiting so that we could drive together to the hotel. A dirty martini, mixed expertly by Rocky, was my companion in the back seat.

The following morning, I went down to the hotel's restaurant. (I'm an early riser by nature.) I grabbed a newspaper and planned on reading through it as I had breakfast. There was a fairly new guy in the league, Chris Conley, and this was his first SEC game with me. Sitting in the restaurant was this guy and his wife, Anna. I introduced myself and visited with them over breakfast. Nice folks.

Anna traveled to most, if not all, of Chris's games early in his career with the SEC. As time passed and life got in the way, she wasn't able to take as many trips. Chris kiddingly said that she only goes to the important games now. Because of this, she is affectionately known as "Big Game" Anna.

We went through our pregame meeting with a little more detail for two reasons: One, it was Chris's first game with us working together; and two, it was the first game out of the gate for the 2003 season. All in all, it was a normal pregame meeting. Chris would be working downfield from me on the same sideline.

We arrived at the stadium on time and began our pregame duties. Part of these involve the referee and umpire going to visit with both head coaches. I think they go to the visitor coach first. The referee asks some cordial, routine questions: "Do you have any trick plays you would like to make us aware of?" "Do you have any questions or concerns for us?" Finally, Rocky tells Steve Kragthorpe, the Tulsa head coach, "I will protect your quarterback throughout the game." In other words, he's going to keep defensive players from taking shots at him after he hands off or passes the ball.

We get the game kicked off without any problems. Arkansas takes control of the game early. The quarterback for Tulsa was their best athlete. He was running a lot because his receivers were being smothered by Arkansas's defensive backs.

Coach Kragthorpe was somewhat quiet on the sidelines. At one point, he did come up to me and say, "Gus, they're pulling our players helmets off!" I hadn't seen anything like that and thought to myself, *Why would Arkansas risk a major foul like this?* Looking back, I did kind of blow him off. But not disrespectfully.

In the second half, it was all Arkansas. During one of Tulsa's offensive possessions, their quarterback took a big hit out in front of me. He had turned up field as a runner. There's no protection Rocky can offer him at this point. As this guy is walking back to the huddle, Coach Kragthorpe starts yelling at Rocky about protecting his quarterback. "Rocky, you lied to me, you lied to me. You said you were going to protect James [Kilian]!"

The next play, they ran a toss sweep to my side of the field. The runner and about four Razorback defenders ended up wiping me out. I came to rest close to the Tulsa bench. It took a couple of seconds for me to get up. As I did, I walked out to the sideline and dropped my flag. Coach immediately starts saying it wasn't his players fault that I got hit.

Rocky comes over and asks what I've got since my penalty flag is laying on the ground. I told him, gasping for air, "Give me just minute." I had the air knocked out of me and I was making sure I hadn't broken anything.

After a couple of minutes, I told Rocky I was okay and that there was no foul. We didn't even give Tulsa a sideline warning. As he was making the announcement that there was no foul on the play, I walked back toward the sideline to a waiting head coach. I reached down, picked up my flag, and while I was putting it back in my pocket, I looked him straight in the eyes and said, "Nobody calls my referee a liar!"

After the game, Chris said he thought I had been killed when he saw me get wiped out on the sideline. He then said he couldn't believe I told the coach not to call Rocky a liar.

Chris got a good lesson in game management that afternoon, though I would have preferred not to take the shot that I did. Welcome to the SEC, Chris.

Early Sunday morning, I grab a cup of coffee and a newspaper before jumping back into the rear of Rocky's rental car for the ride back out to the airport. No dirty martini this morning. But one or two probably would have helped numb the pain from the previous day's hit.

After I settled in, I pulled out the sports section. On the front page was a very large photograph from our game. I moaned out loud, "Oh, shit!" Simultaneously, from the front seat came the word, "What?"

This picture showed two Arkansas defenders tackling a

Tulsa player. A third defender had the quarterback's helmet in his hands. Kragthorpe was right. At least on this occasion he was right and there it was for the whole world to see.

BENDING THE RULES, JUST A LITTLE

Bobby Gaston was the coordinator of officials who took a chance and hired me to officiate in the Southeastern Conference. As it turned out, Bobby and I had some things in common. He knew about these and did something about it.

My children moved to West Point, Mississippi, with their mother in 1997 during our divorce. Being three hundred miles away was very difficult. But I made the best out of it that I could. There was a Best Western hotel in Columbus, Mississippi, that became a second home for me. Over the course of eight or nine years, I stayed there a little over two hundred nights. Sharron Jones, the property manager, always took great care of us.

Bobby Gaston experienced separation from his children as well. He understood the importance of staying in your children's lives as much as possible.

For many years, I was scheduled an unrealistic number of games at Ole Miss and Mississippi State. I could go over on Friday, pick up August and Susan, and spend the extra weekends with them. Sometimes we would even camp out at Lake Lowndes State Park, located just east of Columbus, Mississippi. This was a wonderful place and operated by very friendly people.

The SEC had standing guidelines concerning officials working games at certain schools. For instance, you couldn't officiate games for a school of which you were an alum. If you had an immediate family member that worked at a school, you did not officiate their games. And if you had a son or daughter attending school there, they didn't want you working those games, home or away. The conference was being proactive in eliminating any sense of impropriety.

When my son enrolled at Mississippi State University, I figured my days of working games there were over until he graduated. This turned out to be not the case. I worked many games during his time there. Fortunately, no issues arose.

A few years later, my daughter enrolled at Ole Miss. There had been a change in supervisors. Things changed. I never worked a game there while she was in college.

Not being able to work games there didn't mean my crew wasn't going to Ole Miss. It just meant that officials were switched around and placed on different crews from time to time. Whenever my crew did go to Oxford, my daughter would try to go by and say "Hello" to them.

After she graduated, I resumed officiating for Ole Miss. Oxford is a great town. Two phrases continually resonate from their fans: "We've never lost a tailgate party" and "Ole Miss is the only college in the country where they red shirt Miss America!"

My brother-in-law, Austin Jones, who graduated from Mississippi State, refers to The Grove at Ole Miss as "a thicket."

DON'T GET TRAMPLED

Today, most SEC teams enter the field through a cloud of white smoke and fireworks. At Arkansas, it's just smoke— and a lot of it.

On November 7, 2020, I worked in Fayetteville, officiating the Razorbacks' game against Tennessee. It was a night game, kicking off at just a few minutes past six o'clock. At the beginning of the game, the temperature was in the middle to low fifties and dry. A perfect evening for college football.

Part of my responsibilities as a head linesman is to make sure the home team is out on the field at a certain time before kickoff. This is just a formality because TV is in control of everything. They release the teams onto the field based upon a signal from the producer.

Anyway, back to this game. I'm with the team awaiting our time to go on the field. In Arkansas, they load up all the players in the "Hog Pen." When they open the gate, I normally just step off to the side and let the players run by me. I then walk toward the sideline moving up to the fifty-yard line for the coin toss.

Well, this would turn out to be anything but normal. First, most of the players were in front of me so I couldn't get to my regular spot up front. I tried to move as far to my right as possible, but there were giant players all around me. I would just do the best I could and move in the direction when we were released.

Then the smoke started. Being that it was cool, and the

66

humidity level was slightly high, the smoke was extremely dense and hung like a thick cloud. Soon, I couldn't see anything. Even the player directly in front of me was not clearly visible. It was a really weird feeling, like being claustrophobic.

The players began jumping up and down. *I'm gonna get crushed.* "Just don't fall down," I told myself over and over. When it was time to go, I reached out and grabbed the waist band of the biggest player I could find. I made it out alive. Fortunately, I never had to experience the "Hog Pen" again. "Woooooooo, pig. Sooie! Razorbacks!"

OPPOSITE THE PRESS BOX

I'm certainly no expert on betting, figuring out the odds, covering the spread, or any of that type of thing. I work too hard for my money to risk it on chance. But I am certain about one phenomenon that was consistent throughout my entire officiating career: The visiting team, at all Southeastern Conference stadiums, lose more often than the home team, except maybe at Vanderbilt.

I would place the impact of the home crowd at the top of the list of reasons why the home team wins more often than not. There are probably some other explanations as well.

One additional explanation might be that the side of the field opposite the press box does not get shaded until late in the game, if ever, depending on kickoff time. Every field in the Southeastern Conference is configured with the end zones lined up on the north-south axis. That's every field expect one. The University of Georgia's field is lined up with the end zones in an east/west alignment. They say this happened because someone decided to construct the stadium in a ditch.

Since the beginning of time, the sun rises in the east and sets in the west. If you can keep your opponent in the hot sun for the majority of the game, why not put them on the east sideline of the field? Maybe this would help wear the opponent down quicker.

Because the west side of the stadium would get shaded first, that's where the people attending the games would sit. The press box was put on the same side of the field for the same reason. Plus, it prevented its occupants of having to look toward the sun. The home team also would get some relief from being directly in the sunshine.

In the early years, very few fans were able to travel with their team when they played an "away" game. It cost a lot of money, there weren't many places to stay, and it would take days to complete the trip. It just wasn't practical.

Eventually, as the popularity of the game increased and infrastructure improved, people did start to travel and support their team. As more people filled the stadiums, additional seating was constructed. The fans were segregated into "Home" and "Visitor" sections. Since the home team fans were already established on the west side of the field, the visitor section was put on the opposite side. And they were in closer proximity to their team.

The head linesman's location on the field has traditionally been opposite the press box. The reason for this is very simple. The head linesman is responsible for seeing that the chain crew functions efficiently throughout the game. The line-to-gain equipment, or first down markers, are located across the field from the coaches, announcers, and writers in the press box. This configuration allows for easier visibility to assess the status of the ball during a team's possession. When the chains are placed on the same side of the field as the press box, their view gets blocked by the players and coaches on that sideline.

What does all this have to do with me, as an official? Well, actually, a great deal. Being opposite the press box resulted in me having to deal with a lot of losing coaches. You see, when coaches are losing, they tend to stop coaching and start bitching. That's where your "people skills" are developed.

Also, being on the east sideline subjects you to prolonged, direct sunlight. In early September games, it can be unmercifully hot. There's no relief. Players go in and out of the game. Officials do not. We go every play. It's not unusual to see the officials working on the press box sideline enjoying the shade during the later stages of the game.

There was only one advantage to being on the east side of the field. That would be during a cold, late-season game. At least the sun would help keep you warm and snug during the game. This happened so infrequently that it's simply irrelevant.

Somewhere around 2010, the sideline officials began switching sides of the field. For the first half of the game, the head linesman and side judge would start out on the press-box side. The line judge and field judge would be on the other side. For the second half of the game, they would switch sides.

The most common explanation for this change was that the coaches requested it. Some coaches felt that it might directly impact the actions of the officials. For example, if an official made a certain call on the other side of the field, that official better have the guts to make the same call when he's on the other sideline.

Other coaches took the switching of sidelines as an opportunity to try and intimidate every official working the game, some in the first half and the others during the second half. Whatever.

Most officials approached the changing of sidelines with the wrong attitude. They complained that it interfered with their established routines, or they didn't want to have to deal with a "problem" coach. I, on the other hand, looked at it from a "glass half full" prospective.

The opportunity of being on both sides of the field provided me with the ability to penalize two head coaches during the same game. Unfortunately, this never materialized. If it had, I would have been immortalized as an official. The other officials would have carried me off the field. They would have erected a statue of me. If only some dreams would come true.

THEN AND NOW

Change is inevitable in most everything. It was certainly that way throughout my career. Game assignments and weekend expectations were where some of these changes took place.

When I began officiating, the schedules were sent out to the officials in May for the entire season. It worked well. You could plan well in advance and not worry about unexpected schedule changes. It was nice to know when and where you were going ahead of time. You could save on airfare. Vacations could be planned around open dates.

Toward my final years, the schedule would be released in mid- to late-July. Only the month of September was provided during the first release. Along with this release were the dates you could expect to be assigned a game but not the location. After week one, your assignment for week five or six would be sent. This went week to week until the end of October. The change occurred for a couple of reasons:

The speed of communication and social media had an impact on the dissemination of the scheduling. It did, however, provide a means of switching crews around without anyone realizing that their schedule had changed. For example, let's say a crew has a situation occur during a particular game. It is perceived as negative for the home team. A critical call impacted the game or there was a bad situation with the coaches. Whatever the reason, with the schedules being released in increments, the SEC office could switch crews around without the schools or officials knowing. Only the SEC office would be privy to that information. It actually makes good sense.

Another area that is different involves the hiring and retention of officials. Not too long ago, SEC officials were actively consulted about who would be brought in to work games. The then-current officials would work scrimmages with these prospects. They knew their character and if they had what it took to work in the SEC. This provided a level of comfort and confidence that you had the best officials to work with.

Officials today are primarily hired by the SEC coordinator of officials. The Sun Belt Conference acts as sort of a feeder program for the SEC. There are a few former NFL officials that have a weighted influence in the decision-making process.

In previous years, the Southeastern Conference Football Officials Association was a very proud and loyal group of men. It was extremely close-knit. You looked out for one another. The level of play in the conference rivaled any NFL game. The interest in the South was religious. The NFL was not on everybody's mind.

Now, the SEC officiating program seems to have been relegated to the role of being a feeder program for the NFL. It's still great to be an SEC football official but the extremely high level of pride seems to have deteriorated.

I GUESS WE SHOULD START TRAINING THEM

A man by the name of George Gardner was the supervisor of football officials for the Southeastern Conference from 1948 to 1970. By anyone's measure, Gardner is considered the grandfather of football officiating throughout the country. He devised and wrote the first mechanics manual to be used by all officials. It was his attempt to standardize how all games would be managed. He is one of just a handful of officials that has been enshrined in the College Football Hall of Fame.

One of George's requirements for officials that worked under him in the SEC was to have been a former player in the conference. It was his belief that these individuals would know the game and would call it fairly, even if they were not totally knowledgeable of the rules. It makes perfect sense, and this philosophy was used by several of his successors.

In the early days of football and up until the late 1990s, the training of officials would consist mainly of information being mailed out and read through by those working the game. There would be one or two meetings per year, where members of the officiating association would gather for a weekend and openly discuss how the games would be managed for consistency purposes.

As the game moved into the twenty-first century, there were influences on the game that initiated a steep trajectory of rapid changes to how it was being officiated. The televising of games had the overall biggest impact on the sport. The demographic makeup of the officiating staff was another area that affected how the game was managed.

With more and more games being televised, the scrutiny of officials intensified. It finally reached a point where the physical appearance of the men working the games became an issue. Prior to this, official's only "first impression" was to those coaches and fans in the stadium. Also, the game was being played between the tackles with short runs of three or four yards. This type of play didn't require excellent physical conditioning on behalf of the guys calling the game. As the offensive strategies evolved, the requirements of how the game was being officiated had to be modified.

Along with more games being shown on TV, the technology of the cameras began to improve. There were advancements in the overall production of the game. The flat-screen TV then came into existence. The plasma TV was marketed as "bringing the game into your living room." Now, giant 4K and 8K flat-panel screens provide lifelike views of the game from the comfort of home.

These television changes also provided benefits for officials. Training videos could be put together. Individual plays of interest were recorded and then voiced over to explain what went right, what went wrong, and how the conference office wanted it officiated. In the beginning, one VCR tape was created using multiple recorders. Then, this one tape was duplicated and mailed to each referee during the week leading up to the game on Saturday. Watching the "training tape" became part of the pregame meeting. At the time, it was state of the art. The supervisor of officials, Bobby Gaston, could get the word out to a large group of his officials in a timely manner. Since it occurred weekly during the regular season, officials were kept up to date on rules application, trends in the game and which fouls may not be worthy of calling.

Weekly training videos are still a big part of pregame meetings today. The quality is much better due to digital technology. In addition, every official has a complete file of every play of the game they just completed by the time they get back to the hotel. They log into an account and every game that has been played, up to that point, can be viewed one play at a time. And each file is time-stamped with an assigned play number for reference during the evaluation period.

The other area that affected the management of the game were the officials themselves. One needed change involved where officials were located. For a long period of time, there was a large nucleus located in the Atlanta, Georgia, area. Schools such as Georgia, Alabama, Auburn, Vanderbilt, and Tennessee didn't necessarily have a problem with this. But others like Florida, LSU, Ole Miss, Mississippi State, and Kentucky did. They felt underrepresented due to the lack of officials from *their* area. Impropriety is a word that comes to mind.

In 1992, when the league expanded from ten teams to twelve, the SEC conference office diligently recruited officials from those added areas. Arkansas and South Carolina were the states that these individuals were acquired from. Most, if not all, were officials from other conferences—the Southwest, Atlantic Coast. They had experience, they were familiar with the added schools, and they lived within the footprint of the conference. The nucleus of officials in the Atlanta area began to get smaller.

Somewhere in between the expansion of 1992 and the most recent one of 2012, the requirements for football officials were relaxed. The first major requirement to go was the one requirement of having to be a former collegiate player. Is it possible to officiate football having not been a former player? Sure, absolutely. Does being a former player automatically make you a good official? No, it does not. However, a former player with a natural aptitude for officiating and a willingness to commit to rules and mechanics study makes for a complete and competent official, hands down.

Over the last ten years, the number of former players has been reduced tremendously. There are also other factors being put in place to provide officiating opportunities for those that were previously not considered to work in major college football. Can these people officiate? Sure they can. But a critical question must be asked: Are these the best officials available?

The training videos that were previously mentioned have also gone through some changes other than the technical aspect. Now, a considerable amount of conversation is being used to explain to some officials what is happening on the field during certain plays. For example, if an offensive back is in motion toward the sideline and is not being pressed by the defense, there's really no reason for an official to focus on this player. A former player working the game knows this. A person with limited experience officiating the game now must be taught this.

People really need to question whether the best available officials are calling the game. Or are they content with the outcome for the sake of equity?

THEY DON'T CHECK FOR THAT

Part of being an SEC football official is being cleared by a medical board located in Birmingham, Alabama. There are several components that make up this process.

A physical examination by your personal doctor is the first requirement. The results are forwarded to the examining board.

Another requirement involves a questionnaire that each official is responsible for filling out. This questionnaire determines your risk factors. Risk factors consist of things like the following: an individual's age, whether you are a smoker, if you are prescribed blood pressure or other certain types of medication, and how you performed during a stress test. The number of risk factors determine the steps you must successfully complete to officiate. Younger officials usually have fewer risk factors than older guys. This questionnaire is sent to the medical board.

If you have fewer than two risk factors, you're immediately cleared to the next step. If you have two risk factors, you must complete a stress test every other year. If you have three or more risk factors, you must have and successfully complete a stress test every year. The stress test must be completed by a licensed cardiologist.

The results of your physical examination, your questionnaire, and the results of your stress test, and any subsequent tests as a result of the stress test, are combined and reviewed by the medical board. There have only been a handful of officials that were forced into retirement for not being able to meet the board's requirements.

Once you are cleared by the medical board, you finish the preseason physical assessment by running the timed mile and a half and a brief agility drill. This is done as a group in Birmingham during the summer rules clinic. The time you had to complete the run was based on your current age. I ran the mile and a half twenty-nine times for a total distance of 43.5 miles.

This preseason evaluation is very impactful. It keeps you very aware of your physical conditioning, year round. One of the supplemental officials' life was saved due to this requirement. During his required physicals and stress tests, it was discovered that he had a life-threatening condition he was unaware of. He underwent successful lifesaving open-heart surgery and is still officiating SEC football to this day.

I was able to meet these requirements every year. The only reference to one's visual acuity was on the questionnaire. You would think that one's ability to see would be personally checked by the medical board. It's not. They just take your word based on the answer you put on the questionnaire.

Another thing that amazed me over the years, an official is not checked for color blindness. Do you have any idea how hard it is to follow a brown football being carried by a red or blue jersey against the green backdrop of a football field? I had to train myself to be able to do this. You see, I'm color-blind as a bat.

THE TIMES, THEY ARE A-CHANGING

The head linesman is responsible for documenting fouls during a game and submitting a report of those fouls to the conference office. Over my years in the league, only one thing remained unchanged—well, mostly unchanged. Each official, prior to the season, was supplied with enough physical foul report forms that would be completed during their games. These were carbonless paper forms, originally consisting of four pages. By the time I retired, they had been reduced to three. During a rainy game, you were lucky if you ended up with anything legible.

In the beginning, the process went like this: You took a form with you to the stadium and prayed you wouldn't need two forms. Each form provided enough space to record up to twenty-five fouls. I only had a few occasions where the foul report ran onto a second page. The chain crew had a member who would record the fouls as they occurred. Moving from left to right across the form, the information recorded was

> *Quarter, Time on the clock,*
> *Offense/Defense/Kickers/Receivers, Type of foul,*
> *Accepted/Declined/Offset,* and the *calling official(s).*

Most of the individuals who charted these fouls did a decent job. My only request of them was to please write so I could read the information. No hieroglyphics.

At halftime, I would take the form into the locker room with me. I would briefly go over the form to make any corrections, additions, etc. During our postgame meeting, I would do the same for the second half.

At the conclusion of the game, the person charting these fouls was responsible for delivering one of the bottom pages to each head coach or his representative prior to leaving the field. I would get the top two pages—generally, the most legible.

If I had flown to the game, I would take time on the flight home to create a clean report on a new form. If I drove, I would wait to do this after I got home. The top area contained space to write the date of the game, the two teams playing, the location of the game, kickoff time, whether the game was on TV, start time, end time, total time, whether the game was suspended and, if so, for how long, and a list of all the officials working the game by position. I would take one copy and put it in an envelope addressed to the SEC office in Birmingham.

On Monday morning, I would drop the envelope in the mail. It always amused me that by the time the report got to Birmingham, any controversy had subsided as teams were well into preparing for their next game. But that's how we did it.

The paper form is still in use on the sideline to this day. However, all data is entered electronically by the head linesman. My new laptop was a tax deduction. I did my best to have the final report submitted by the end of our postgame meeting. I would add each foul as we were led through the debriefing. There were areas in the electronic form that allowed for descriptions of fouls. For instance, there are various categories of pass interference. An official may have had a foul for pass interference and add that it was an "arm bar."

One would think that with all the technology in today's world, the paper form would have gone the way of the dinosaur. Seriously, the times, they are a-changing.

IT WAS LIKE
THE WIZARD OF OZ

I drew Vanderbilt at South Carolina during week three of the 2013 season. I've taken hits in games before but none like the one I would take that night.

Under Armour had begun providing us with our uniforms right around this time. I decided to wear a pair of their shoes with fairly long cleats, since we were going to be playing on natural grass. They were like old-school shoes.

With three minutes left in the second quarter, South Carolina was up, 24–7, over Vanderbilt. The Gamecocks had the ball on their own twenty-yard line with second down and three yards to go. They threw a swing pass into the flats in front of me. I was moving down the sideline as the ball was caught by the Carolina receiver. Just after he caught it, a Vanderbilt defensive back hit him and drove him straight back toward me. My first thought was, *Oh, shit. I'm going to get hit. Move back!* As I planted my right foot for leverage, a player stepped on my foot, driving my new cleats into the ground preventing me from getting out of the way. To make matters worse, one of the chain crew members didn't move out of the way, as they are always instructed to do.

I took a direct hit from both players. When I came to, I had four or five trainers leaning over me, calling my name. I had no idea where I was, only that I was lying on grass. I remember them having a hard time removing the earpiece of the communication system. About nine minutes later, they wheeled me off the field to the locker room. Mike Shirey took my place and Marc Curles came off the clock and worked the line judge position. I have no idea who worked the clock.

Things were so confusing. It turns out I had suffered a severe concussion. To this day, it all seems like snapshots. One moment, I was getting loaded on the cart to take me off the field. The next, I'm wondering why the assistant commissioner of the SEC, Greg Sankey, is standing in the evaluation room with us. Over the next couple of days, I was able to piece together what had happened.

I remember just prior to getting hit. The trainers got to me in unbelievably quick time. James Franklin, the Vanderbilt head coach, cleared the team area around me. Clint Haggard, the head athletic trainer for South Carolina, took control of the situation and coordinated the care I received.

They put me through the concussion protocol tests. I failed miserably. At one point, they had me close my eyes while I was standing up. They caught me before I hit the floor. I remember telling everyone that I've got to get word to my mom that I'm okay. All I had to do was give them a number to call. I couldn't recall any numbers. They handed me a cell phone anyway. Out of habit, I was able to press the right sequence of numbers that belonged to my daughter, Susan. When the phone began to ring, I handed it back to Greg Sankey. He assured my daughter that I was okay, and he was counting on her to let the rest of the family know. My daughter now had the future commissioner of the SEC's personal mobile number.

I was kept in a dark room. They were always assessing my condition. Holly Rowe came in to check on me. She let the world know that I was going to be okay, but that I had a severe concussion.

There was a TV in the training room with the game on. I kept looking at it thinking, *If I'm not in the van when the game is over, I won't get back to the hotel.* A decision was made that instead of going to the hospital, I was to be taken back to the hotel where someone would stay with me through the night. These decisions were not mine.

With about five minutes remaining in the game, they began taking me back to the van. I got there just before the game was over. When the clock hit zero, within seconds the other officials, one by one, began piling into the van. After everyone was accounted for, we rolled out of the parking lot under police escort with blue lights flashing. I had to close my eyes as these lights were making me extremely nauseous.

I don't remember the postgame meeting. I don't remember talking on the phone that evening to anyone.

There was no way I could drive. How was I going to get home?

The next morning, Clint Haggard and the team doctor showed up at my room. They put me through more tests and told me the concussion was bad. Unknown to me, my brother-in-law, Tom Meyer, was on his way to Columbia from Atlanta to drive me home. He's a retired Delta pilot so he was able to make a flight into Columbia.

I ate some breakfast and saw a few of my other crewmates as they departed to go home. When Tom landed, he called to say he was going to get a taxi and come to the hotel. Clint told him to wait there, and he would come and get him.

I don't remember much of the drive from Columbia, South Carolina, to Cumming, Georgia. I do remember how glad I was to be home. I don't remember if the lady I was dating at the time came over to check on me. For some reason, I don't think she did.

Early in the afternoon, Steve Shaw called to check on me. He was the coordinator of football officials. Not long into our conversation, he said, "You don't remember talking to me last night, do you?"

"No" is all I said.

I called my primary physician, Dr. Thomas Tucker, and told him what happened. He already knew. I was instructed on things I could and could not do. How was I going to run my business? Thankfully, Lana was working for me then and she took care of everything.

Two weeks later, I worked the LSU at Georgia game. I almost got hit on the opening kickoff. I never should have worked that game. Somehow, I made it through without really messing up. During the game, however, the referee had to shut the game down and make an announcement that they had to restart the play because "the head linesman was not in position." I was doing the best I could.

So, here's the weirdest thing about whole situation: When I was knocked unconscious, I had a very vivid dream. I dreamt that I was weed-eating in my front yard back home. I then started hearing voices and I began looking around the yard to see if I could locate who was yelling at me. I was walking around and then just sat down on the lawn. It was at this point that I came to and saw all the people standing over me back in Columbia, South Carolina. I felt like Dorothy at the end of *The Wizard of Oz*. It couldn't have been a dream 'cause you were there, and you were there, etc.

It took about nine months for me to fully recover.

WE DON'T WANT
THAT CALLED

On October 12, 2019, I worked the Alabama versus Texas A&M game in College Station, Texas. This was an enjoyable trip for a several reasons. College Station is a great town, the detour to the Blue Bell ice cream factory never disappoints, and I had a childhood friend and his wife in town for the game.

Dale and Wendy Vaughan live in Ovilla, Texas, just a two-and-a-half-hour-drive south of College Station. I was able to get an extra room at the same hotel that the officials use. They got the whole experience of what officials do over the weekend, minus sitting in on our pre- and postgame meetings. Other than that, they saw everything. Particularly, the after-game rituals of the crew.

Kyle Field is an exceptional football facility. Large is an understatement. The fans play a very big part of the total experience. But in this game, it was all Alabama. A&M just couldn't match up.

It was during this game that I realized just how much college football had changed during my career. And in my opinion, for the worse.

Late in the third quarter, there was a Texas A&M pass play over toward the sideline I was working on. The offensive player ran what is called a swing pass slightly downfield. As the receiver and defensive back are running side by side, their legs get tangled, and they both go to the ground. There's nothing to call. I look downfield to the side judge, and he's shaking his head "no" while giving an incomplete signal. I'm right in front of the Alabama team area on the sideline.

The Texas A&M receiver, while sitting on the ground, thinks it's defensive pass interference and starts moving his right arm as though he's throwing a flag. You see this often during games.

Instead of getting up and going back to the huddle, this Texas A&M player runs toward me and, when he gets close, says, "You f**king suck!" I put my flag on the ground for an unsportsmanlike-conduct foul against him. I report the foul to the referee, and he makes the announcement. We step off fifteen yards against Texas A&M and get ready for the next play.

During SEC games, sophisticated two-way radio systems are used so that officials can talk to one another during the game. The replay officials are also using the same equipment. Suddenly, through my earpiece, I hear the replay officials calling my name. "Hey, Gus, Birmingham wants to know what the player said to you."

I replied, "I'll tell you after the game."

Then I hear, "No, they want to know now." I repeated what the player told me. There was no more communication the rest of the game concerning this particular play.

During SEC football games, there is a group of individuals in the video center at the conference office in Birmingham. They provide an additional layer to the replay process. This is referred to as collaborative replay. There are former officials, video technicians, the supervisor of officials, and upper-management personnel of the SEC.

We finish the game and return to the hotel to get cleaned up and go through the postgame debriefing. At the beginning of the meeting, our observer begins telling us about his conversation with the staff in Birmingham concerning the unsportsmanlike-conduct foul. We were told, unequivocally, that they do not want that called in the future.

It was then that I realized that it might be time for me to consider the timeline for my retirement. I didn't make a big deal out of it but made it clear that if a player cussed me like that again, the conference would have to go in one of two directions: defend me or fire me.

That decision never had to happen. I got out in the nick of time.

AIR GUITARIST EXTRAORDINAIRE

The sound systems in the stadiums throughout the SEC are magnificent. While working on the field, the noise seems to float above your head. It's almost as if you're immersed in music.

The volume emanating from the loudspeakers is well beyond anything you will experience from your home entertainment system. Human bodies in the stadium affect the sound. They absorb a lot of the reverb that exists in an empty stadium.

Some institutions are famous for playing certain songs at the same point in their games. One prime example occurs at the Georgia Institute of Technology. No, they are not an SEC member. Used to be. But still, if you've ever been in their stadium during the third and fourth quarter break, you know what the Budweiser theme song means to the student section.

The University of Tennessee had a similar tradition for several years. During their third and fourth quarter intermission, they would play "Gimme Shelter" by the Rolling Stones. On the field, it sounds unbelievable. It sounded even better when there were not a lot of fans in the stadium. And this happened from time to time. Tennessee was struggling in the win column at that time. The crowds usually began filing out of the stadium in the third quarter. Adding some reverb to this song, at the volume they played it, caused the music to pour out over the field.

During one particular game, the crowd had pretty much emptied during the middle of the third quarter. After we completed our administrative responsibilities during the quarter break, *the song* began to play.

The last two plays of the third quarter resulted in a touchdown and a successful try by the visiting team. The first play of the fourth quarter was going to be a kickoff with Tennessee receiving the ball. The referee is positioned in the middle of the endzone and I'm standing on the goal line to his left.

Jimmy Buffett has a song that talks about a certain feeling coming over him. Well, I had this same feeling come over me! I wasn't afraid of anything. I was a fearless man.

The referee is trying, inconspicuously, to get me to stop what I'm doing. He is frantically shaking his head from left to right with a terrified look on his face. He also has one hand below his waist shaking it as if he's telling some little kid to knock off whatever he was doing.

No one has ever played an air guitar like I did on that night in Knoxville on the field of Neyland Stadium. Those fans that left early will never know what they missed.

OUR CHURCH IS THE COOLEST

The Southeastern Conference administrators and officials receive and send most all information through a dedicated website, the URL of which will remain secret! It contains everything related to football officiating. Your schedule, the directory, weekly tests, memorandums, and the portal to file game reports are just some of the sections.

When you log in, as is normal, you land on the home page. At the top of this page is an area where you can submit famous and/or inspirational quotes. These rotate and change each time you log in.

One Monday evening, I had received an email that the next segments of my schedule had been released. After logging in, a quote that I had never seen before popped up. It was from the young son of one of our officials, who at the time was living in Starkville, Mississippi. A smile came over my face.

"Our church is the coolest. It's right next to the football stadium!" by Luke Freeman.

Family and Football

DON'T BE IN A HURRY

My father officiated football in the Southeastern Conference too. That's not why I did it. As far as I knew growing up, it was just something he did. There were no games on TV where I could watch him. I didn't travel with him. As vice president of Royal Crown Cola, he was required to travel, a lot. When the fall rolled around and football started, I hardly ever saw him.

When I started officiating middle and high school football, I began to understand why he loved it so much. You were around your friends that came from all walks of life.

As my career began to develop and the SEC was showing interest in me as an official, my dad began to talk with me in regard to what I was doing. We finally had a unique common denominator between us. It just worked out that way. He didn't interfere at all. He just observed.

He would drive up from Sandy Springs, Georgia, to Cumming often. We would go to lunch and visit. It was great. I didn't grow up with this, so I had a real appreciation for it.

The first two years I spent with the SEC, I worked most as an alternate, running the game clock. That's just the way it was back then. I expected nothing more. It served as a probationary period.

At the beginning of my third season, things were different. I had been assigned five games on the field. I was excited beyond words. I had really made it.

After I got my assignments, I called my dad and gave him the rundown.

"Great. Let's have lunch tomorrow. I'll meet you at Po' Folks around 11:45." Cumming didn't have many restaurants in the early '90s.

Once we were seated, we talked for a few minutes and ordered. After the waitress left, he reached into his pocket and pulled out a little box. He slid it across the table and said, "I want you to have this." It was his SEC officiating ring. He wore it all the time. My dad was a big man. There was no way I could wear it without having it resized. I sincerely thanked him. "You've done this on your own. You should wear it now."

Dad didn't get into my officiating business but one time during my career. He didn't have to. He knew as much about it as anybody did. He did, however, give me what turned out to be the best advice anyone ever gave me regarding officiating: "Don't be in a hurry. Get there early and stay a little late. Enjoy it while you can, it'll be over before you know it."

THE DAY MY DAUGHTER WAS BORN

On February 27, 1993, I had a scrimmage in Athens. Ray Goff was the coach of the Bulldogs at that time. He held spring practice early with the thought being that if any player got injured, they would have a little extra time to recover before summer practice started. Made sense to me, but it didn't make the weather any warmer. Georgia had no indoor practice facility then.

My children's mother, Joan, was close to nine months pregnant with our second child. We had just gotten our first cell phone the previous Christmas. As I was packing my bag for the practice, I made sure the phone was fully charged. This model was referred to as a "compact unit." However, it was still the size of about two decks of playing cards.

Before I left, Joan told me she felt okay but not like usual. "I can call you if anything happens." Out the door I went for the hour-and-fifteen-minute drive from Sugar Hill, Georgia, to Athens. Her mother had also come over a week or so earlier from Woodville, Mississippi, to help.

As I was getting dressed with the other officials, I told them that we are just about at our due date and that Joan felt a little bit different that morning. Jimmy Harper told me to just go on back home. They would work the scrimmage without me. No problem. I showed them the cell phone and that I would have it on the field with me. Cell phones were not all that prevalent in 1993. Particularly among young couples starting out.

About forty-five minutes into the scrimmage, the phone

rings. Fortunately, we were in a break during the practice. When I answered, the person on the other end was my mother: "Joan's water broke, we're on our way to Northside Hospital. We'll see you when you get there." Northside was, and still is, the baby factory of Atlanta. They were following the plans that had been put in place over the last couple of months.

I told Jimmy Harper that "it was time." My car was parked under the east end of the stadium. I took off my striped shirt and jumped in for the drive to the hospital. It was about noon.

When I parked at the hospital, I grabbed my bag and went inside. Other than a solid black shirt, I'm in my full-blown SEC officiating uniform. I was hard not to notice. The receptionist directed me to the room where Joan and my mom were. After I took a quick shower and dressed, my mom wished us well and went home. She only had a ten-minute drive through Sandy Springs.

At this point, her water had broken but there were no serious contractions. A couple of hours later, the real contractions started. Things were beginning to happen. When they got more intense, the epidural was administered. That's a big friggin' needle.

Once that procedure was completed, the pain Joan had been experiencing diminished. But so did the rate of her dilation. Things began moving at a snail's pace. It's now about 10:30 p.m. There's a lot of activity due to the labor and delivery nurses coming in on a regular basis checking on her progress.

I'm starving. I hadn't had anything to eat in over fourteen hours. I found a snack machine, and the nurses brought some drinks from their breakroom. We're just waiting. Things are not moving along very fast.

Around four o'clock the following morning, things went from around ten miles an hour to a hundred. Two nurses came in the room. "We got to go. Here, put this on. Place your personal items under the gurney and follow us." They handed me a yellow paper jumpsuit with matching shoe and head covers. I ended up putting on the jumpsuit backward. I've been up for almost twenty-four hours and suffering from malnutrition.

We were in the operating room very quickly. I was just an observer at this point. Joan was being prepped for surgery. It was amazing to watch how everyone functioned as a team. I was asked about watching the surgical procedure. I'm sure they didn't want to be picking me up off the floor in case I fainted. I went back and forth from talking with Joan to watching the surgeons. It was an amazing experience. When they began to reach in to remove the baby, Joan asks me, "Are they touching me? I feel pressure." *Uh, yeah. The epidural was doing its thing.*

"It's a girl!" exclaimed the doctor. We had chosen not to know what the sex of the baby was. Our son had been born almost six years before. Having a daughter? Wonderful. We had already picked out her name: Susan Elizabeth.

Two other medical people were brought in right after the delivery. They were respiratory therapists. Susan was not getting the necessary amount of oxygen she needed. They re-assured us that everything would be okay. At that moment, she went from blue to pink. They finished cleaning Susan and Joan was being taken care of by the delivery doctors. The two individuals who were working on Susan told me to come with them. "You can go up to your wife's room after she leaves the recovery room." It's now about five o'clock Sunday morning.

As I was walking with the two people pushing this incuba-tor contraption, the male respiratory therapist asked me, "You don't know who I am, do you?" I'm thinking to myself, *Well, hell no. I've been up for twenty-four hours, I'm starving, y'all just saved my daughter's life, and all I can see are your eyes.* I simply replied, "No."

He pulled down his mask and it was Rusty Warren. I had gotten to know him through my roommate at Millsaps College. Rusty and Jody had grown up in the same Mississippi Gulf Coast town, Long Beach. Rusty was going to school at the Mississippi Medical College. I almost panicked. This guy was an absolute party animal in college. After witnessing his lifesaving work and combining that with my memories of him, I was very confused. How could somebody make that kind of progress in life? Yes, there's always hope.

We couldn't visit much at all. They were immediately called to another operating room. I thanked them and said "good-bye." I've never seen him since.

Susan was taken into the nursery and checked out. A nurse picked her up and draped her across her left arm. She then took what looked like a rubber spoon and began to beat the snot out of her, literally. She must have sensed my alarm. She pressed a button by her station and, over this little speaker, tells me, "She'll be fine in just a minute. Don't worry."

Everything was fine. I visited with Joan and we both needed sleep. They were going to keep Susan in the nursery for a while. I went home and slept like a baby myself. Around four o'clock Sunday afternoon, my mother-in-law woke me up so I could drive back down to the hospital. It took me a few minutes to realize that it was still the same afternoon and not the next morning.

They brought Susan into the room shortly after I got there. I held Susan for a while and then laid her in my lap where she fell sound asleep. The nurse commented on how calm Joan and I were with the new baby. We were. Susan slept through every night after that.

We went home on a Tuesday, March 3. Four days later, the blizzard of 1993 hit. We knew it was coming. I had stacked all the firewood on the deck by the back door. Propane cookers were set up in the garage. We had plenty of water and food. We were ready.

The storm started on Saturday morning, March 7. I had never experienced thunder snow. Fifteen inches of snow later, it quit. We only lost power for about thirty minutes. Joan's father had driven over from Mississippi. Her mom had already been there for three weeks. Our little three-bedroom house was getting small. Her parents were a big help, but it was nice to be home with just the four of us after they left. August was as good a big brother as any sister could have. And still is!

DON'T MAKE ME BREAK YOUR HEAD

My daughter, Susan, graduated from high school in the spring of 2011. Shortly after graduation, she enrolled at Ole Miss and began summer school classes. She's one of the few people I know that is doing today what she wanted to do as a young child. Being a labor and delivery nurse has its challenges, but she loves it. Toward the end of 2023, she'll be a licensed nurse practitioner.

Prior to the 2011 football season, I made my way to Oxford, Mississippi, on a Friday afternoon, to work a scrimmage at Ole Miss. This trip also provided me with some time to visit with Susan. She and her roommate met me at the stadium the following morning and stayed for the scrimmage. It was interesting watching Susan act so matter-of-fact around her roommate. She was very comfortable around the officials and coaches.

There were nine officials available to work the scrimmage, so there were various opportunities for me to switch out to talk with Susan and her roommate. Susan knew where they could be on the field so that they wouldn't be in the way or risk getting hurt.

During one of the breaks, I walked back toward the bench area to get something to drink. As I was moving behind the players' area, I noticed three players standing together. It was obvious that they were gesturing something about my daughter and her friend. Not wanting to miss an opportunity, I eased over to the side of this small group of players. One was definitely a giant offensive lineman with the other two being receivers or defensive backs. I asked #72 if he knew the girl in the blue shirt, being that he was the biggest one. As all three of them looked at me with uncertainty in their expressions, this enormous kid says, "Yes, sir."

My reply was simple. "Don't make me break your head!" And then, I just walked off. Behind me I heard sounds of disbelief of what they just heard, including, "Oh, shit, he just called you out right here in front of everybody." The two other players were rolling with laughter.

After the scrimmage, Susan waited for me to get cleaned up and dressed. We went out to dinner that night and visited before I dropped her back at the dorm.

Early the next morning, Sunday, I drove back home. Sometime Monday around lunch, my daughter calls. After the normal, "Good mornings," etc., the rest of the conversation went something like this:

Susan: "Why did you tell Jonathan that you were going to break his head?"

Me: "That's not what I said."

Susan: "Well, what *did* you tell him?"

Me: "I said 'don't *make* me break your head.' There's a big difference."

Susan: "Oh, *okay.*"

Obviously, word of my encounter with #72 spread around campus pretty quick. I don't know if this had any direct effect, but Susan never had any problems during her time at Ole Miss.

IT'S REALLY BAD

Early season games in the South have a high probability of being delayed by thunderstorms. Travel to and from game locations can get disrupted particularly when flying. You never take the last flight out if you can help it.

Idaho opened at Florida on September 1, 2014. After a four-hour weather delay, we lined up for the opening kickoff with the Gators receiving the ball. After a sixty-eight-yard return, play was suspended again. Total number of plays for the game: one. But that's not what this story is about.

The state of Mississippi can have bad storms in September. In 2005, I had an early season game at Mississippi State. The game was threatened by thunderstorms all night. One never got close enough for play to be suspended. It wasn't on TV, only radio. Imagine that today.

In the second half of the game, I took a direct hit to my left knee from a player. It immediately swelled up and I had to come off the field. The trainers determined that nothing was broken or torn so they wrapped it in ice. The officiating crew made a switch: I went to the sidelines and ran the game clock while the alternate took over my position.

After the game, I called home, as I normally did. My wife, Cheryl, and I chatted for a while about the game and life, in general. I never mentioned that I had been hit. There was no need to cause unnecessary worry. I was bruised but not broken.

I left for home earlier on Sunday morning than I had originally planned. There was a dangerous line of storms drawing a bead directly on Starkville, Mississippi. A tornado warning had been issued. I made my ritual stop at Shipley's Donuts for a blueberry muffin, smoked sausage roll, chocolate milk, and a large coffee. I then pointed the car east and started my drive home. After passing through Columbus, Mississippi, and crossing the state line heading toward Reform, Alabama, I looked in the review mirror. All I can see are black, ominous clouds. The pressing thought running through my mind was, "You shouldn't have stopped at Shipley's!"

About that same time, my cell phone rings. It's Cheryl checking in on me. The first words she asks is, "How bad is it?" Not "Good morning" or "How long have you been on the road?" I told her, "It's really bad, I'm going to try to make it without having to pull over. I just don't know where I would go."

There was a long pause of complete silence on the other end of the call. Cheryl then asked me, "Why didn't you tell me last night?"

My dad had called her just prior to the two of us talking that morning. He asked her if she knew how I was doing after getting hit the night before.

It turns out we were talking about two separate topics in the same conversation. I thought it was funny. She didn't hold the same opinion.

SOME KIDS CAN
SLEEP ANYWHERE

The year was 1999. My daughter, Susan, was six years old. I had a double header on Saturday of this particular weekend. Ole Miss had their spring game first, followed by Mississippi State having theirs later that afternoon. It's an hour-and-forty-five-minute drive from Ole Miss to Mississippi State. I picked Susan up from her mother's house in West Point, Mississippi, on a Friday afternoon in April. My son, August, had plans and didn't go with us. Susan and I drove to Oxford, Mississippi. We checked into our hotel and went out to dinner. After dinner, we got ice cream before going back to the hotel for the evening.

On Saturday morning, we got up, dressed, and went down to the lobby where we made waffles for breakfast. As Susan was finishing up, I checked us out of the hotel, and we headed over to Vaught-Hemmingway Stadium for Ole Miss's spring game. They were scheduled for a noon kickoff.

Susan had already figured out how things worked, and she took great pride in being able to hang out on the field while I did my thing. During warm-ups, she came up to ask me if I would introduce her to David Cutcliffe. Coach Cutcliffe had been hired by Ole Miss the previous December to become their head coach.

I took Susan by her hand and walked out on the field. I couldn't take a chance on her getting hit by any player! We approached Coach Cutcliffe, and I told him that my daughter wanted to meet him. It was amazing. He dropped down on one knee so that he was on eye level with her. He then extended his hand to her and said, "Hello, I'm David. What's your name?" They talked for a good three or four minutes and then he excused himself telling her that he had to go to work. He didn't have to treat her like that, but he made her feel so special. The sign of any good coach!

The spring game started, and Susan stayed well away from the sidelines, as I had instructed her. When the game was over, I took off my shirt on the way to our car (even at spring games, some people just don't care for officials). We immediately took off to Starkville, Mississippi, for the spring game at State. We stopped and got chicken strips somewhere in the middle of nowhere. We drove in silence for a while. It's hard to eat and talk at the same time.

We arrived at the stadium with about ten minutes to spare. State had finished their warm-ups and were lingering around the team area. Susan *didn't* ask to meet Jackie Sherrill. You know how those Ole Miss people are!

The same routine was followed by Susan during this game. She stayed away from the sidelines. When we finished the game, I was looking around for Susan and didn't see her. Panic didn't immediately set in, but I was wondering, *Where could she be?* About that time, one of State's trainers pointed her out to me. "She asked me for a towel a little while ago. She's asleep under the bushes over there behind the table with the Gatorade on it."

We had dinner and ice cream that night too. She was asleep before we got back to the hotel. I dropped her off at her mom's house on Sunday morning and drove home, reflecting with pride about how she handled herself over the weekend.

TELEVISION GRAPHICS

For most of my career, I worked on the field opposite the press box. As a head linesman, one of my responsibilities was coordinating the chain crew. The chains, or line-to-gain equipment, were placed on that side of the field for one main reason: it was easier to see them from the press box. If they were operated on the same side as the press box, the press would lose sight of them among the players and coaches blocking the view.

When games began to be televised, the audience could see for themselves what the down and distance was. The chains were always at the top of the screen, which is where I was located during the games.

Because I was at the top of the screen, usually all anyone could see of me was from my waist down. I've got stocky legs, and people could identify me by how I stood.

Many years ago, I mentioned to my daughter, Susan, that I was going to a lunch meeting. I told her that there would be a man there by the name of Bob Rathbun who was going to talk about announcing college football games. Bob had announced several games that I had worked in.

Bob and I got to be friends somewhere around 2007 or 2008. I was asked to meet with Bob one day for lunch. The purpose of the meeting was to help him better understand the rules of the game. He had been broadcasting basketball for most of his career. Bob is currently the TV announcer for the Atlanta Hawks.

For a few years, Bob and I would meet, go over new rule changes. We would talk mechanics and why we, as officials, did what we did. He wanted to know how replay was designed and the steps we took during the review. He wanted to learn all he could to be the best announcer he could be. I truly admired his effort.

Before I left for this lunch program, Susan told me she wanted me to ask Bob a question for her.

"Sure, no problem," I said. "What is your question?"

"Can they put the graphics at the bottom of screen?"

I wasn't exactly sure what she was referring to, so I asked could she be a little more specific? She began to explain the box they put at the top of the screen that shows the down and distance, score, time outs, and all that stuff. I didn't have a problem with asking Bob that question for her, but I asked her why. Susan told me, "It covers you up and I can't see you some of the time."

After lunch had concluded at this meeting, Bob was introduced and began his presentation. At the end, he opened things up for questions. I took the opportunity to ask Bob my daughter's question. He commented about how astute my daughter was for asking that question. The next game I had where Bob was the announcer, the graphics were displayed at the bottom of the screen.

THE CHANT

I have many nieces and nephews. Most are on my ex-wife's side. However, I still think of them as family. Many of them attended schools where I officiated games during their time in college. At one game in Oxford, Mississippi, I had an unusual situation occur.

We had completed our pregame duties—the coin toss was done, and we got the football game off to a good start. One of my nephews was a first-year student at Ole Miss at that time. He was sitting with his fraternity brothers in the student section. During the first half of the game, it sounded as though someone was yelling my name. The side judge heard the same sound. After listening to it for a few minutes. It became a very distinct chant: "Gus, Gus, call one for us!"

This continued for the better part of the second quarter. Lo and behold, whoever Ole Miss was playing that day jumped offside, and I put a flag down on the field. The student section erupted. But at least the chant stopped.

Fortunately for me, the foul also drew flags from two other officials, so no one could say that I was being partial toward Ole Miss.

Thank you, Kyle, for that moment of recognition.

CHRISTMAS ALL-STAR GAMES

Christmas of 1996 was a difficult time for me. My kid's mom and I had separated during the previous summer. We had agreed that our son and daughter would stay in Cumming, Georgia, for Christmas and then they were going to their maternal grandparents' home the next day. That didn't materialize. My wife's mother drove to Cumming to take them back to South Mississippi for Christmas.

I'm not exactly sure how he found out, but Ray Moon got wind of my predicament. He called about a week before Christmas and asked me what I was doing over the holidays. After explaining that I wasn't exactly sure what I was going to do, he told me, "You're going to work the Blue-Grey All-Star game on Christmas Day. You don't need to just sit at home."

My mother and father lived in North Atlanta about twenty-five miles south of Cumming. Since they were out of the country for Christmas, I decided to go down to their house and spend Christmas with one of my older sisters, Suanne. Our first cousin Louis was there with his partner, Gerry.

Around 3:30 on Christmas morning, I woke up, dressed, and walked upstairs in the house to get ready for my drive to Montgomery, Alabama. Suanne was waiting for me when I came up. We wished each other "Merry Christmas" and I was then out of the door.

My parents' house was located just off I-285 on the north end of the perimeter. As I started driving, I immediately noticed that there were no other cars on the road. Just me. I drove around the west side of Atlanta and picked up I-85 South just past Hartsfield-Jackson International Airport. I finally saw another vehicle about ten miles south of the airport. *They must be delivering a surprise Santa gift for Christmas,* I thought to myself.

When I reached Newnan, Georgia, I pulled off the highway to get another cup of coffee. There was a little gas station open and, certainly, they would have a fresh pot. The lady wished me "Merry Christmas" as soon as I walked in the door. "What are you doing out so early?" She felt sorry for me when I explained where and why I was going. I assured her that it was a good thing. We exchanged Christmas greetings as I left the store to continue my drive. I was way ahead of schedule.

When I reached the end of the entrance ramp, I pulled over to the side of the road. I grabbed my cup of coffee and sat on the hood of the car waiting for the sun to come up over the horizon. I had a lot of emotions running through my mind but, overall, I was in a good place. Still, I thought, *So this is what soon-to-be-divorced college football officials do on Christmas morning.* When my cup was empty, I jumped back in the car and started driving toward Montgomery.

I met the rest of the crew at the hotel in downtown Montgomery. Everyone, except me, had arrived the day before. We ate breakfast and talked for a couple of hours. There would be no pregame that day. If you didn't know what to do after all these years, well, tough luck. Basically, we were just going to be ball chasers. The game was more about the players showcasing their talents than that of a team winning or losing.

The teams were made up of players from all over the country. It was the North versus the South all over again. The designated "home team" wore dark jerseys, and the "visitors" wore white ones. Each player wore their school's helmet. It was a different experience officiating the game. The players talked with each other during the entire game.

Rom Gilbert was the referee, and Ray Moon was the head linesman. I worked as the line judge. I don't recall the rest of the crew, and there's no game assignment for me to go back and reference or any YouTube replay.

The other officials' wives were able to hang out on the sidelines during the game. They could come and go as they needed to. It was a very casual atmosphere.

The stadium was mostly filled with the parents of players and a few local residents. I remember there being a lot of young kids there. I believe the bowl committee donated tickets to area charities so they could provide opportunities for underprivileged children on Christmas Day.

During the first commercial break, I looked across the field and noticed Ray had walked over to the stands and was smoking a cigarette. He was kind of backed under the seating so no one would see him. When we came out of the break, he was standing on the sidelines ready to go. This happened during each time out we took throughout the game.

At some point in the third quarter, we went into a normal TV time out. When I looked across the field this time, there was Ray signing programs for several of the little kids that were hanging over the railing of the stands. He was acting like a true celebrity. And, it was pure Moon at his finest.

I have a program from every bowl game I ever worked except the two Blue-Grey games. Each of the other twenty-plus programs are framed and in my basement. The only thing I have to remember the games by are two sweatshirts. I guess something is better than nothing.

After the game, I showered in one of the other officials' rooms and headed back to Atlanta. Instead of going to my parents' house, I went to Mary Jane and Sterling Bennett's. They were hosting a Christmas dinner and had invited me to come by earlier in the week. Suanne, Louis, and Gerry were going to be there, also.

My cousin Louis, an accomplished executive chef, and Mary Jane prepared a spread of food that was unrivaled. The highlight of the dinner was a congealed crabmeat salad. It was very different, but delicious. At some point during the dinner, someone commented about how good the "crabmeat Jell-O" was.

The food, wine, family, and friends made for a great conclusion to a very unusual Christmas.

MY LADY FRIENDS

July is a very busy month in the period leading up to the start of every SEC football season. The 2009 annual summer preseason clinic started on July 23 and finished up on Saturday afternoon, July 25. It's during this phase that a symbolic transition from preparation to execution takes place.

Your physical conditioning is at its peak, or at least it should be, and the rules have been studied intensely. During the summer clinic, there is the physical assessment that measures just how good of shape individuals are in and there is a rules test to determine the results of your study efforts. After several days of coordination meetings, it's time to move toward getting the season started. Officials begin to go to campuses and work practices with the teams around the league. Eventually, Labor Day weekend arrives, the games begin, and it's time to put into action all the things you've done to prepare for the season.

Around this time in 2009, I experienced something out of the blue that couldn't have happened at a better time. From a personal relationship standpoint, I was very single. There were the occasional dates but a special someone was absent in my life. A long relationship had recently ended, and it had created a big void for me. Officiating was providing a lifeline during this period, as it had done at other times during my career.

On the morning of Sunday, July 11, the house phone rang. I normally wouldn't answer it because the only real reason I had this number was for the alarm system in my home. Since I was standing there, I answered it. Surely on Sunday morning, there wouldn't be a telemarketer or political campaigner on the other end. I picked it up saying, "Good morning, this is Gus." A sweet voice replied, "Gus, this is Wanda from down the street. It's Pam's birthday today and I wanted to invite you to come down and have brunch with us."

I most definitely was not expecting this. I had gotten dressed that morning and was heading to church. Wanda called me just as I was walking out the door to get in the car. I made a quick decision to take her up on the invitation. Ten minutes later, I was greeted by this very petite, elderly lady. "Well, good morning. So glad you could make it." A wonderful friendship had started, and I didn't even know it.

Wanda introduced me to her daughter, Pam, for whom the brunch was being held. There was another couple there. Their names were Scarlett and Tom. They were very nice people.

The house was quaint but very well kept. Everything looked like it belonged exactly where it was. Wanda escorted me out to the small screened-in porch. In one corner of the porch was a linen-covered oval table that was covered with a multitude of appetizers. The first impression I had was that this could be something out of *Southern Living* magazine. It was a beautiful work of art. Not long after seeing this, I discovered that Pam and Wanda were very accomplished chefs.

I had not met Wanda or Pam other than the casual wave while passing their house when I was on the way home. This had gone on for two years. They were out in their yard frequently and it was nice to always get enthusiastic reactions whenever we saw each other. Now, I had names to put with faces.

From that Sunday morning on, we became friends. They invited me to countless dinners. Dr. Dunn, a very interesting elderly gentlemen, would join us on many occasions. He didn't have that special someone either. His wife had passed away several years earlier.

Many times, I would stop and visit Pam and Wanda if they were out in the yard or sitting on the front porch. We would enjoy each other's company for hours. I always felt welcomed, and our friendship was effortless and greatly appreciated.

We checked in on each other from time to time. When the weather would get bad, I tried to make sure I reached out to them and make sure they were okay. I had an old four-wheeler and could get out of the neighborhood when it iced over or snowed. I could get provisions for them if they needed anything. When I would have to travel out of town for more than a day or so, Pam would get my mail for me. She would do this when she would take her dog, Pookie, out for his daily drive around the neighborhood. Pookie later passed away and left a huge void in Pam and Wanda's life. We just kind of helped each other out in one way or another over the years.

At one point during my officiating career, I worked out under the guidance of a personal trainer. Being that Pam and Wanda were excellent cooks, I persuaded them to provide meals for me. With recommendations from my trainer, I would get meals and snacks delivered to my house every afternoon, Sunday through Thursday. It would start with a hot dinner for that evening. There was homemade cereal for the next day's breakfast, a mid-morning snack followed by a meal for lunch and a mid-afternoon snack. This routine repeated itself for about six or eight months. I was spoiled rotten.

I had a fairly large flock of laying hens at my house for many years. Pam had gotten back into doing some catering. She needed eggs; I needed chicken feed. We concocted a super easy agreement. When she needed eggs, she would put her empty basket on my front porch. The next morning, I would fill up the basket, which normally consisted of about three dozen eggs, and place it on her front porch on my way to work. In return, she would bring me a fifty-pound bag of chicken feed about every four weeks. It worked: I got rid of eggs, she got fresh eggs, and the chickens stayed fed.

Our friendship grew over the years. We could count on one another, and we did. There were times where we helped each other where only true friends could and without hesitation. Details are not necessary but trust me when I say that if I ever need anything, I know who I can count on. We're not all up in each other's business, and we will go stretches without talking with one another, but it doesn't affect our friendship whatsoever.

Pam and Wanda really weren't college football people. However, they were intrigued by what I did when I would take off for the weekends during the fall. They would pepper me with questions that I enjoyed answering. Soon, I was required to make sure they knew which game I was going to work, what time kickoff was, and what channel they could watch it on. It was more that they were watching me! I found out that they would have phone calls with their friends and family leading up to and during my games. They were the leaders of my own personal fan club. They performed this task admirably.

Pam, Wanda, and Dr. Dunn were together watching my game at South Carolina when I got knocked unconscious. Dr. Dunn knew it was serious when he saw the hit. He comforted Pam and Wanda. Knowing that they would be watching the game, I called them when I got home to let them know I was okay.

I have cooked periodically for my crew when we've had games close to my home. I would drag along my cookers so that I could fry catfish and chicken in the parking lot of the hotels to avoid going out to restaurants. On one occasion, I asked Wanda if she would make me a tray of potato salad. Enthusiastically, she put together one of the best recipes for potato salad a group of officials would ever eat. My crew members were made aware of just who prepared it. They are the ones who nicknamed Pam and Wanda my "Lady Friends." Wanda took great joy in telling other friends of hers how she helped me in feeding my crew.

I had our crew take a group photo in front of the spread of food. I took a framed copy of the picture and gave it to Wanda for her birthday. It was easy to remember when she was born because it was on Groundhog Day, February 2. She spoke of that picture from time to time.

On June 12, 2022, Wanda passed away. About a week and a half prior, I had sat on her front porch and had a wonderful visit. Mentally, she was still very acute. Physically, she was frail and weak. She cared for me dearly and I loved being around her. I miss her each time I drive by their house.

Pam and I still take time to visit. During the time when Wanda was being taken care of in the house by a hospice group, there was a major water leak in their kitchen. As if caring for her mother wasn't enough, this was put on her shoulders. Maybe it was for a reason.

Pam has another dog now by the name of Ollie. Fortunately, Wanda got to know Ollie before she left us. Pam and I visit from time to time. We still talk a little bit about football but not like we used to. Now we talk about our neighbors and other things we never got around to before. Mostly, we just make sure each of us are doing okay.

BLUEGRASS CHOCOLATE-CHIP COOKIES

Ben Oldham was an official in the Southeastern Conference for many years. He worked as a deep wing (what is now known as the field judge). I had a chance to work a few games with him earlier in my career.

Ben lives in Lexington, Kentucky, with his wife, Mel, who travels with him on numerous occasions. After Ben retired from the field, he worked as an observer and then became a replay official. A couple of years ago, he retired from the game altogether.

For over a decade, Mel would bake chocolate-chip cookies and deliver them to the hotel where the officials working the Kentucky games would stay. These weren't ordinary cookies. They were absolutely the best chocolate-chip cookies, hands down. It had precisely the right amount of chocolate chips and nuts.

When she delivered them, they weren't just thrown in a bag. There were many individual bags that held six fabulous treats. Each bag was meticulously sealed with a gold-foil twist tie. Even with the whole crew eating them, there were enough for Friday evening after dinner and Saturday afternoon after the game.

Many officials just took them for granted, as if they had just fallen out of the sky. Anyone who has watched someone bake homemade cookies—not those from a tube—knows that it is a labor of love. I, for one, enjoyed each and every cookie knowing that the person who made them cared about each official as though they were her own son. Thank you so much, Mel! Oh, by the way, my mailing address is—!

IT SOUNDED LIKE THUNDER

My son, August, started to become a Mississippi State fan in 1997. The following year, State played a game in Stillwater, Oklahoma. I was assigned to work the game and I was able to take August with me. He was eleven years old.

We flew into Oklahoma City on Friday evening, picked up our rental car, and drove to the hotel. We decided to order pizza and have it delivered. When it arrived around eleven p.m., I woke August up so we could eat. I'm not sure he was totally awake, but eat he did, and then he fell right back to sleep.

The following morning, we went downtown prior to driving over to Stillwater. After finding a place to park, we walked over to what had been the Alfred P. Murrah Federal Building. Three years had passed since Timothy McVeigh and Terry Nichols set off an explosion, which killed 168 people, destroyed about half of this building, and were responsible for an estimated total loss of $650 million.

It was an extremely emotional stop in our trip together. More so for me. I was in Winder, Georgia, on my way to work a scrimmage at UGA when news came over the radio that the explosion had occurred. Now, we were standing on the actual grounds where it happened. The memorial chairs made me cry. Particularly for the little children who perished. Mississippi State's band was there also. Normally a lively group, they were equally overcome with emotion and hardly a word was said between them.

When it was time to go on to Stillwater, we headed to the

car talking about what we had just experienced. During our drive, I reminded August that the father of his childhood friend, Kyler, was from Stillwater, Oklahoma. His dad, Scott Case, lived across the street from us in Sugar Hill, Georgia, and made his living playing football for the Atlanta Falcons and Dallas Cowboys.

We met the other officials at their hotel just a little after noon. The restaurant was closed, and we didn't have time to go and pick something up to eat prior to our pregame meeting. I also discovered that the family members that were going to make the trip had decided to stay home. I had no one for August to sit with during the game. This was a problem. I couldn't turn an eleven-year-old loose in the Cowboys stadium alone.

Fortunately, I ran into a former teammate of mine from Millsaps College. Melvin Smith was an assistant coach at Mississippi State. He was able to get me a sideline pass for August. This took some work on his part. Understanding my situation, he did what he needed to do and was able to pull it off.

After our pregame meeting, with August in attendance, we left for the stadium. We changed into our uniforms at the stadium, which is different from what we typically do at SEC schools.

August was starving. I mentioned I would try to get him something when the school liaison came to check on us. Overhearing the conversation, Mike New, the back judge on the crew, asked him if he liked vienna sausages. His eyes lit up and he said "Yes, sir!" Mike had saved the day. Over the next twenty years, whenever I saw Mike, he would give me a can of vienna sausages and tell me to give them to August.

Oklahoma State beat Mississippi State like a drum that afternoon. August survived being on the sidelines. He didn't get lost or hurt.

After the game, I got showered and dressed while August

visited with the other guys. We said our good-byes and head-ed back to Oklahoma City for the night. I carried him up to the room and put him in bed.

The next morning, as we were driving to the airport for our flight home, I asked him what he thought about the game. He told me if he ever hears "First Down Cowboys" again, he's going to throw up. He then tells me that the players sounded like thunder when they ran by him.

I agreed and then my thoughts raced back to the Murrah Federal Building. It must have sounded like thunder there, also.

TWENTY-SEVEN MINUTES

There are some things that are not included in the operations manual of life. You just have to figure things out and make it happen.

For much of my working career, I fixed cars and trucks. It wasn't a prestigious profession, but it was steady and recession-proof. Plus, I made a hell of a lot of money doing it. I worked for various people and other businesses before striking out on my own. I had customers from all over North Atlanta, including my mother and father.

My dad was having some problems with his Ford truck and asked me to look at it. It was just as easy for me to come and pick it up at his house, plus I would get to visit with my mom. On a Thursday afternoon, after work, I jumped in my car and drove to Sandy Springs, Georgia.

After our visit, I brought his truck home with me, leaving my car for him to use the following morning. My parents had a second home in Highlands, North Carolina, and my dad had plans to go up there over the weekend. He was going to bring me my car, pick up his truck, and drive to Highlands when I had the truck ready to go.

I went into work early the next morning to see what problem he was having and do what needed to be done to repair it. It ended up being something minor. It was ready to be picked up anytime on his way to the mountains. Not long after he picked his truck up, leaving my car with me, he called wanting to know if I had found a set of his keys in my car or office. I looked in both places while I had him on the phone. No luck. In return, I told him I had misplaced a bank deposit I had put together and to look in his truck to see if I had left it there. The keys weren't located, nor were the checks that needed to be put in the bank.

Dad and I talked two more times over the weekend, prompted by his wanting to know if I had located his keys. He volunteered that he hadn't seen any checks either.

Monday morning came and I had a call on my work phone from Dad.

"Did you find my damn keys?"

"No, and I guess you don't have any checks for me?" He didn't.

"I'll call you tonight after I get home" was the last thing he told me before he hung up.

Running a small, specialty automotive-repair business kept me very busy all day long. After talking with my father, I had to leave and go pick up a part that had been special ordered. I incorporated this with my normal daily loop through town. This loop included stopping by the post office, going by the bank, and any other business that needed tending to. I was back at the shop within thirty minutes. The loop was small on this particular Monday morning.

I handed off the needed part to one of my employees and turned to go into my office. My secretary/service manager, Shirley Pruitt, came out immediately and handed me a piece of paper with a name and telephone number on it. This wasn't unusual, I had calls coming in all day long. But she had a sense of urgency in her voice. She said I needed to call this man right away. It was very important that he talk to me.

Because we were always out in the shop or parking lot, we had cordless, portable phones. Shirley handed me her phone, so I didn't have to go into the office and get mine. The man's name was Jim Terry. He and my dad were both involved with the Bobby Dodd Coach of the Year Award. I knew of Jim, but

I had never spoken to him. He answered the phone on the second ring.

He began to tell me that he had been talking to my dad about the upcoming vote for the Dodd Trophy, but suddenly, the call dropped. That's not unusual in that area of North Carolina. He then told me that about five minutes later, he had gotten a call from the chief of police with the Highlands Police Department. My dad had been taken to the emergency room at the hospital in Cashiers, North Carolina. "You need to call this guy, let me give you his number." I wrote the name and number down in the palm of my left hand.

I thanked Jim and told him I would call him back as soon as I heard any updates about Dad.

I quickly called the number that Jim had given me. A gentleman answered and told me that my dad had been taken to the emergency room at the hospital in Cashiers, North Carolina, not far from Highlands. I asked this guy what happened.

He explained that they had gotten a call about a medical emergency in downtown Highlands. The EMTs and other rescue personnel had found my dad unresponsive in the driver's seat of his truck. He had parked in front of a restaurant close to the Olde Edwards Inn. They were able to get him out of the truck, began administering CPR, and took him to the hospital. "I found his phone and called the last number shown in the call log." Jim Terry's number was the last call on Dad's phone. I have thanked God on numerous occasions that it wasn't my mom's number.

The chief of police had the number to the hospital and instructed me to call them when we hung up. I thanked him for his help and told him I needed to make the next call.

The hospital in Cashiers is not very big. When the receptionist answered, I explained who I was and why I was calling. "I need to put you on hold. I will get the doctor as soon as possible. Don't hang up."

I had a roommate from college drown one summer—this sequence of phone calls and instructions was eerily familiar to what I experienced twenty-four years earlier.

A doctor came on the line, and I told him who I was and why I was calling. "Your dad was brought in a little while ago. He was in bad shape. We did all we could. I'm sorry to have to tell you but your dad didn't survive." Though completely shocked, I asked him not to tell anyone else until he heard back from me.

I had to get to my mom and give her the news. I found Shirley and briefly told her what had happened. "Handle the shop the best you can. I'll check in when I can, but I have no idea when that will be. I've got to go tell Mom what has happened."

Shirley teared up, gave me a hug, and told me she loved me. "If you need anything, let me know." I left, running on pure emotion.

I stopped by my house, walked in, and the first words out of Cheryl's mouth were, "What's happened?" I told her that Dad had just died, I needed to get to Mom so I could tell her what had happened, and would she please stay home by the phone in case I needed her to make calls, etc. It was the one decision I made that day that I have regretted ever since. She wanted to be by my side, and I didn't let her do it.

The drive to Sandy Springs takes about forty minutes. Two things needed to happen: One, I had to figure out what I was going to say to my mom and, two, I had to call my four sisters and break the news to them.

What could I possibly come up with to tell her? I'd just deal with it when I got there. Calling my sisters was my priority during the drive.

I called them in birth order, moving down from the oldest to youngest. One by one, I made my calls. Every sister answered the phone the first time I dialed their number. I was calm, to the point, and asked them not to contact Mom until they heard back from me. All of them were in disbelief. Upon hearing what I was telling them, three handled it as best they could. But one completely lost it. I stayed on the phone with her until she promised me she would not call Mom until after I was able to get to her house. Mom didn't need to be alone when she found out that her husband of fifty-five years, had passed away.

I had been able to let all my sisters know what had happened. Now I just had to tell Mom. I pulled around the back of her house, parked the car, and walked into the eating area of the kitchen.

"Hey, Mom." She wasn't alarmed. "What are you doing?"

She replied, "Your dad wants meatballs for dinner tonight."

I walked over to the stove, turned off the burner, and slid the pan to the side of the stove. Now she was alarmed. I sat her down at the kitchen table, held her hands, and said, "Dad's not coming home for dinner."

I gave her a few minutes to let the news sink in. I then slowly began to tell her what I had been able to find out. Suddenly, she grabbed both of my shoulders and said, "I told your dad never to die during Christmas!" The date was December 10 and my dad had been in full-blown Christmas mode since Thanksgiving. The house was completely decorated, and all his "odd" mechanical holiday adornments were in place. He was Santa Claus to so many people.

We both fell silent sitting at the kitchen table for what seemed to be a long time. Above the door leading into the den was one of Dad's Christmas clocks. Every hour, on the hour, it would chime a Christmas carol.

It was now two o'clock in the afternoon. The clock chimed "Silent Night." My dad was present in the kitchen with my mom and me.

The rest of the afternoon was a blur of my sisters coming to the house and me taking my parents' address book to make "the call" to their friends. I called Georgia Tech and inter-rupted a meeting Dan Radikovick was in to inform him. Dan was Tech's director of athletics. He said he would, and did, handle everything concerning Tech. By now, telling folks was kind of like going through the motions. But I knew I needed to be as calm and reassuring as possible when I passed along the news.

In between making calls, I leaned back in my chair to take a short break. Just then, the phone rang. When I answered, I heard, "George, this is Lucius [Lucius Sanford]." When I broke the news to him that Dad had died, he broke down and cried. He loved my dad. He wore the same number as my dad when he played linebacker at Tech. Reluctantly, I told Lucius I had to go and continue making phone calls. It's hard to hear a grown man cry.

I had done all I could that day. Family and friends were at the house. There was plenty of support for Mom. I needed to go home and check on Cheryl. I had talked with her several times during the day. But I was ready to get home.

Somewhere on Georgia 400—which runs north, away from Atlanta—it hit me. Who was I going to talk to now that Dad was gone?

For a couple of reasons, I decided to make a quick stop by my office. Shirley had the shop totally under control, but I wanted to see if I needed to return any phone calls. Mainly, I just wanted to be by myself for a few more minutes.

By habit, I checked the phone's call history. I scrolled all the way to the point where I had last talked to my father and then I moved forward from there. I got to the point where Jim Terry's number showed up.

I had called Jim back later that afternoon as I said I would. During that call, Jim told me how he had gotten in touch with me. He didn't have my number, but he knew he needed to talk with me and not call Mom after speaking with the police chief.

Jim explained that he called Kent Keesler in Chattanooga, Tennessee, who was a good friend of my dad's. Kent didn't have my number, but he told Jim he would try to get it and call him back as soon as possible.

Kent hung up the phone and called the Southeastern Conference office in Birmingham. Meagan Patterson was filling in at the front desk that day, answering the main switchboard phones. Meagan had been Bobby Gaston's assistant for years until she became the mother of twin boys.

Kent explained the situation and, because of my relationship with Meagan, she gave him my work number. Kent then turned around and called Jim back with my contact information.

All of that took place between the last call I had with my dad and the first call Jim made to my office. And it only took twenty-seven minutes.

When I got home, Cheryl was waiting for me. I still shouldn't have left her there alone. I'm sorry. I spent a long time telling her about the calls to my sisters, the clocked that chimed, and how short the period of time passed between me last talking with my dad and Jim Terry calling me.

We both fell asleep realizing that it was a God thing for sure.

Gallery

HALFTIME

It's been a tradition for decades that the bowl committees present watches to players and officials. This Culligan Holiday Bowl was my first "official" bowl game. By the end of my career, I had worked a total of sixteen bowl games and five SEC Championship games. My watch collection sits proudly in my home office.

Many great memories were made during our times around the tracks. Over twenty-eight years of official runs, I ran a total of 168 laps for a distance of forty-two miles. The mile-and-a-half run is no longer part of the official's annual assessment. My twenty-eight runs for a distance of forty-two miles is a record that will stand the test of time.

It's not often that three alumni from the same high school get to work an SEC football game together. Though we were from different graduating classes, we did get to work the "Fan-Hurling Championship" game with one another. From left to right: Bill Bowdoin, Bert Ackerman, and I all graduated from Marist High School in Atlanta, Georgia.

The 1996 Auburn versus Alabama game in Birmingham was my first Iron Bowl. Back row, L to R: Bill Stanton, Ben Oldham, Bobby Moreau, Butch Lambert Jr., me, and Billy Beckett. Front row, L to R: Rogers Redding, Paul Petrisko, and Steve Shaw.

Even though it had been twenty years since I had to penalize Coach Spurrier in Baton Rouge during the Florida at LSU game, there was still an icy reception when I arrived to work one of his scrimmages in Columbia, South Carolina. I guess old coaches never forget.

I was off the Saturday of October 24, 1998. My fiancée and I rented a lone house on a three-acre island near Harbour Island in Eleuthera. I overpacked.

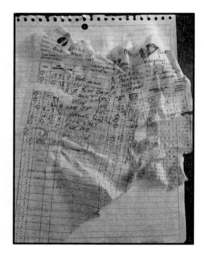

Foul reports for SEC games are the responsibility of the head linesman. A multicopy form is given to an individual on the sideline who enters the information during the game. After the conclusion of the game, the information is entered into an online form for the conference and the NCAA. One form is from my first game and the other is from my last game. It was a steady downpour during my final game in Baton Rouge. The form had to be pieced backed together.

My daughter, Susan, would hang out at the scrimmages that I would work when she was in school. Practices were usually followed up with a nice dinner on the square in downtown Oxford.

My son, August, and I flew out to Oklahoma City in September of 1998. Both of us were starving when we got to Stillwater for the game. Mike New came to the rescue with a giant can of vienna sausages and crackers.

Bill Goss is not a golfer, but he can let his golf cart roll off into a creek. Ray Moon and I were called over, as if we could make it magically disappear. When we got there, he tells me, "We need a picture of this for the Golden Whistle Award!" We didn't even get wet!

Skip Ramsey is one of the funniest people I know. I heard him tell the same joke at a Hooter's one evening at least five times. When he was asked to tell it for what would be the final time that night, he requested that every Hooter's waitress be lined up in front of him. It was a beautiful site.

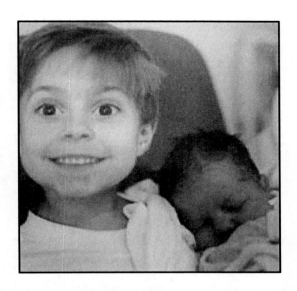

August and Susan went with me to San Antonio while I was assigned the Alamo Bowl. August was really into photography at the time and Susan was getting aggravated with him taking so many pictures of her. The situation created a "Proud Father" moment.

I don't have very many pictures of my father and me together. However, this one is my favorite. We were at the Piedmont Driving Club in Atlanta. The Bobby Dodd Celebrity Golf Tournament was being held that day. My father, George Morris, and Kim King, the young lefty from Georgia Tech, founded this event. To date, the tournament has distributed over one million dollars to Atlanta charities over its twenty-eight-year history.

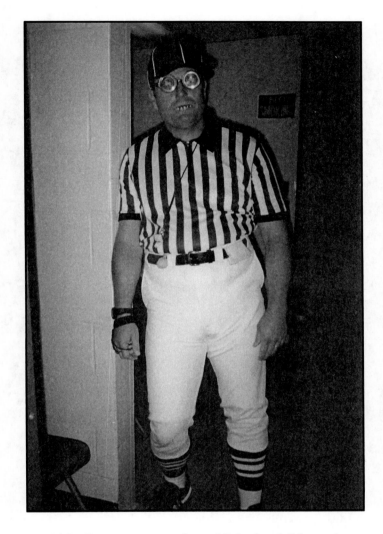

Eddie Powers put on these "Coke bottle" lens glasses and the "Bubba" teeth just as the representatives from the Motor City Bowl walked into our dressing room. The look on their faces was priceless.

Working in Baton Rouge was always a pleasure. You could always count on eating well. Also, Coach Miles always seemed to have something up his sleeve. During a game against South Carolina in 2007, he pulled off a perfect fake field goal and ended up winning the game, 28–16.

The final Blue-Grey All-Star game was played on December 25, 2003. This Christmas Day classic originated in 1939 and was played in Montgomery, Alabama. Besides a minimal game fee, officials were given an "official" Blue-Grey All-Star sweatshirt.

SEC officials wear high-end communication equipment in order to talk with one another during the games. Each official is fitted with a custom earpiece prior to the season starting. Chris Conley didn't have his yet when we went down to Auburn for a scrimmage. When he expressed concern about the generic earpiece falling out, I found a roll of duct tape that eliminated his worry.

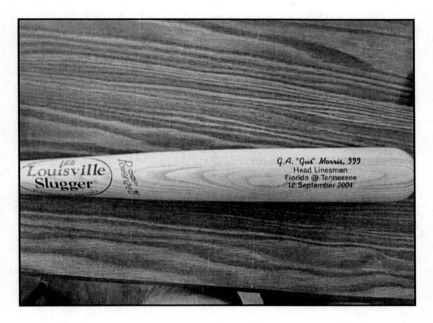

In 2004, the crew I was on was really having a tough year and taking a beating from many angles. We had really screwed up a game at Tennessee in September and the rest of schedule was very tense. In hopes of easing some anxiety, I ordered seven custom engraved bats from the Louisville Slugger company.

Consider me "old school" but I found three-quarter-high cleats and the Acme Thunder whistle to be a highly functional combination. Yes, I got ridiculed often. However, real aficionados of college football appreciated my effort.

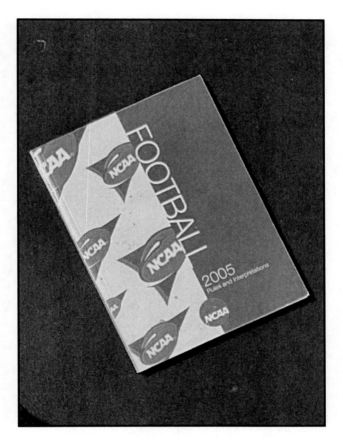

Studying the rules always took a lot of effort for me. Penalty enforcement and what are referred to as exceptions to certain rules are what challenged me the most. In the current climate of college football, rule changes occur every two years. This process minimizes the chance of any change creating unintended consequences. The exception are rules regarding player safety.

Somethings have more sentimental value than others. This ring means very much to me. It's not the fact that my father wore this ring often before he gave it to me. Each time I wear it, I go back to the day that we had lunch together when he gave it to me. It was a private transfer of tradition. He placed great pride on what was taking place.

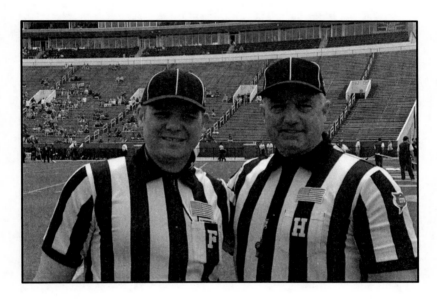

Brad Freeman was one of my favorite young officials when he was coming up through the ranks of the SEC. His father, Steve, and I had worked together in the league before he moved on to the NFL. It wasn't long before Brad followed his dad into the NFL after a great SEC career himself.

Almost every official in the SEC gets a nickname attached to them. I think I had three during my thirty-one years in the league. After sixteen years, Russ Pulley and I will still send pictures where the number 205 shows up somewhere. It's been seen in mailbox numbers, screenshots of game clocks on TV, gas prices, and various other forms.

Paul Petrisko and I go back to a Georgia Tech versus Georgia freshman game in 1989 or 1990. We introduced ourselves to each other under the stands of Grant Field in Atlanta early on Thanksgiving Day morning. We instantly became friends that would stand the test of time. We worked a tremendous number of games together and traveled many miles in each other's company. We spent so much time together that he earned the nickname "Paulette."

I owe a great deal to Ray Moon. He was there when I needed a friend and, more importantly, some support. When Ray passed away, I drove over to Birmingham for his funeral. During the service, the pastor was talking about Ray and how she got to know him during his long illness. At one point, she said there were times where Ray would make her blush. Knowing Ray as well as I did, it became apparent that not even a woman of the cloth would deter him from telling one of his signature jokes.

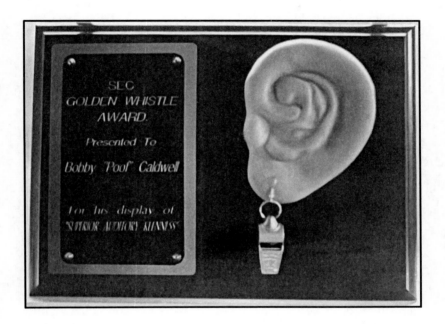

I was awarded the Golden Whistle award during the summer clinic of 1995. It was my responsibility to make the award the following year. The winner of the 1996 Golden Whistle award was Bobby Caldwell. Because of the "award show" I put together, Bobby made a motion that I become the permanent presenter of the award. I made a total of twenty-five presentations, the last coming during the virtual clinic of 2020.

Mike New and I were moved from the SEC scrimmage roster to the active roster at the same time. We worked many, many games together in our early years. Shortly after we got to know each other, he started calling me "Trey." I thought to myself, *Is he losing his mind? Surely, he knows my name is Gus.* As it turns out, he tagged me with my first SEC nickname. From a family name standpoint, I'm a third (III). "Trey" was short for being a third.

Scuba diving is considered risky by a lot of people, including crewmates. However, with the proper training and safety measures, it can be unbelievably relaxing. Now that I'm retired, it's time to brush up on my certifications and increase my dive time.

There's something about a good, cold beer after working a game for three-plus hours. It doesn't matter if the weather is hot or cold. Early kickoff times were the best, as far as I was concerned. It provided plenty of time during the afternoon and evening to hang out with my crewmates before heading home the next day to start a new work week.

The Christmas season is my favorite time of year. Prior to working the Orange Bowl in 2017, I was driving through the square of my home town, Cumming, Georgia, and ran into the real deal. We slipped inside the local pharmacy for a photo op. I had just signed closing documents on a business I was selling. All was right with the world.

This all started at the University of Tennessee when they were hosting Alabama. For the next couple of years, they would ask if I wanted hotdogs. After that, warm hotdogs, with my name written on them would be in the locker room when we arrived for the game. The University of Alabama followed suit and "dogs" would be waiting on me when I arrived. My crewmates knew not to mess with them.

It's said that you're lucky to have five friends you can really count on. Pam and Wanda most definitely fall into that category. You know you have something special when you get together and there is never a lack of things to talk about. I never took that for granted. Wanda appreciated a picture of my crew where she had made a tray of potato salad for our pregame meal.

Bobby Gaston took faith in my abilities and hired me as a football official for the SEC in 1990. His wife Gail insisted he make the decision. Over the years, we had our ups and downs together. No matter the circumstances, he always had my best interests in mind. He went to bat for me several times when I really needed him to. A bond was formed, and we became great friends. At ninety-nine years old, he still plays a short round of golf almost every day. I love the man!

Saturdays in the South

The 1998 Holiday Bowl

I worked my first bowl game in 1998. It was the Holiday Bowl in San Diego between Nebraska and Arizona. Frank Solich was coaching Nebraska and Dick Tomey was the head man for Arizona.

I had already scheduled to take a week off from work between Christmas and New Year's prior to this bowl assignment. Cheryl, my fiancée at the time, and I spent just about the entire week in Southern California. Nice place to visit but I wouldn't want to live there.

As bowls go, I got spoiled with this being my first one. The liaisons for the officials, which are assigned through the bowl committee, where absolutely the best. They had three major events scheduled for us. The first was a sunset cruise on a private yacht around San Diego Bay. It was very nice. Plenty to eat and drink. And that, we did.

The following day, they took us out on the naval yard. This day made an impact on me that still brings tears to my eyes. After clearing security, we drove over to where the submarines are docked. There were two of them for us to tour. Each person or couple was assigned a sailor during our time aboard the submarine. I'm guessing ours was eighteen or nineteen years old.

We spent about an hour inside the submarine *USS Alabama*. It was the same submarine used in the film *Crimson Tide*. I guess being SEC guys, it was a little ironic. We learned that every area is designed to function in multiple roles. For example, the mess area (dining room) also serves as the surgical and triage area if needed. But everybody knows how to fight fire!

There were some things that we could not see or know, due to being highly classified. Some stuff was covered up with brown paper sheets. It was made crystal clear that we were not to even attempt to see what was hidden. And I mean crystal and "loaded weapon" clear.

Toward the end of our tour, we were gathered and taken back up and out of the submarine where we disembarked. Just when everyone got on the dock, a lone whistle blew somewhere on the other side of the harbor. Everything stopped—and I mean *everything*. Each sailor immediately faced the nearest flag and snapped to attention, rendering an extended salute. Simultaneously, every flag, as far as the eye could see, was being lowered. I cannot express the sense of pride I had swelling up inside of me. There were many misty eyes in our group, mine probably the most.

Later that evening, our third event was a wonderful dinner at a beautiful restaurant with an ocean view. I can't even re-member what I ate due to the experience I had had earlier in the day. *USA, USA, USA.*

The day of the game finally arrived, and we did what we were out there to do. We, as officials, did fine. No issues. However, there was one play that ended up being kind of a big deal.

Toward the end of the game, Arizona scored to take the lead. Right after the touchdown, I had a flag down for a dead ball, personal foul against Nebraska. Don Shanks, the side judge, had a flag down for another dead ball, personal foul against Arizona. During those years of NCAA football, you penalized dead ball fouls in order of occurrence. So, we penalize Nebraska half the distance which was one and a half yards from the three-yard line, and then we penalize Arizona fifteen yards the other way. Arizona had planned to go for two points from the three-yard line, but their penalty put them back on the sixteen-and-a-half-yard line. They kicked the extra point but a field goal by Nebraska would have tied the game. Never happened.

The next year, dead ball, personal fouls by each team that occurred as ours did, became offsetting fouls. Dick Tomey was on the NCAA rules committee, and they make the rules, not officials.

I'M THROUGH

The Iron Bowl, played between arch-rivals Alabama and Auburn, is one of the most anticipated games in the country. It's the last regular season game for both teams and played on the Saturday following Thanksgiving. The game was played on Legion Field located in Birmingham throughout most of its history. The Auburn faithful felt like this was an annual de facto home game for Alabama. The 1989 game was finally played in Auburn after much insistence. The year 1998 was the last time the Iron Bowl was played in Birmingham. Now it's played on each school's campus, with Auburn hosting on odd-numbered years.

My first experience with this game was in 1996. The Crimson Tide was the designated visiting team this year. The officials stayed at the Sheraton hotel in downtown Birmingham, across the street from the SEC office. The fire alarm was set off three times during the night before the game. Each school accused the other of being the culprit. Either way, it was a long, restless night.

Gene Stallings was the head coach at Alabama and Terry Bowden was in the same position for the Tigers. There were rumblings that Coach Stallings may retire after the game.

The excitement surrounding the stadium was absolutely electric. At the time, Legion Field held about eighty-three thousand fans. It was packed to the rafters.

Just prior to the first half kickoff, an Alabama drill team member got knocked over by some members of Alabama's Million Dollar Band. This delayed the start of the game for several minutes. Seeing what had happened, Coach Stallings began walking down the sidelines toward the endzone where the young girl was being administered medical aid. As the official closest to that sideline, I went with him to be able to signal to the referee when we were clear to start the game.

When Coach Stallings reached the girl, he dropped down on one knee and took her hand. He assured her that everything was going to be okay. He brushed back her hair and wiped the tears from her cheeks. Once she was on her feet, he again provided reassurance to her. His actions deviated from the hardcore perception most people held of Coach Stallings, particularly mine.

As we walked back up the sideline to get the game underway, I heard him ask, "Gus, do you know how lucky we are to be doing this?" Immediately, I thought to myself, *He's setting me up!* But indeed, we were very lucky.

It was a very intense ball game. At some point in the third quarter, Coach Stallings asked me how I was doing and if I wanted some water or anything else. Now, I'm thinking he's really setting me up.

With about a minute left on the clock, Freddie Kitchens, Alabama's quarterback, threw a pass to Dennis Riddle for the game-tying touchdown. The successful extra point put the Crimson Tide in the lead. The crowd noise caused by the touchdown and extra point literally took my breath away. This was the first time that I had experienced that level of excitement from the fans in the stadium. It shook the ground I was standing on.

There was slightly less than one minute to play in the game. ESPN took their last commercial break. Auburn still had a chance. While standing on the sideline waiting for Alabama to kickoff, Coach Stallings was standing next to me. We were just waiting for the Red Hat to clear the field so we could get the game going. After a minute or so, he told me, "I'm done." I slowly turned to him, shook his hand, and thought to myself, *Of all the people watching this game, I'm the only person who knows he's retiring.*

Coach Stallings's last regular season game was a win over his arch-rival, 24–23.

THAT DEFLATED FEELING

Tennessee's 2017 game against the Minutemen of the University of Massachusetts looked like the beginning of the end for Butch Jones. His first three games of the season were not spectacular performances by his team. They did beat a bad Georgia Tech team, 42–41, but still needed double overtime to do it. An FCS school, Indiana State, came to Knoxville and was beaten, 42–7, by the Vols.

Florida was their next opponent at home and Tennessee suffered its first conference loss of the season. In fact, the Volunteers didn't win a conference game in 2017.

My crew was scheduled to work in the Tennessee versus UMass game in Knoxville on Saturday, September 23. With a noon kickoff, I could drive home after the game and be there by eight o'clock.

The week prior to the game, Steve Shaw had emphasized during the weekly training video that we really needed to enforce the rule that coaches could not come out on the field and protest a call, period. *I can do that*, I thought to myself. I usually had good control of my sidelines and could mostly avoid this type of situation.

Tennessee was just not playing well. There was no score by either team in the first quarter. Halftime saw the Volunteers leading only by a score of 14–6. UMass outscored Tennessee, 7–3, in the second half. Tennessee was able to hold on to a 21–13 win. UMass should have been nothing more than a speed bump in this game. In the second quarter, Tennessee called a time out while they were on offense.

The Minutemen had forced the Vols into a third-and-long situation.

The SEC Network was broadcasting the game. During this particular time out, they went away for a commercial break. The Tennessee offense came over to the sideline area to meet with the coaches and discuss strategy. I would normally position myself close to the huddle and in view of the timer indicating when we would resume play. As I'm standing there drinking some water, Coach Jones comes around my left side breaking clear of the huddle and toward Matt Loeffler, our referee. Jones then imitates the holding signal toward Matt, simultaneously yelling, "They're f**king holding!"

Opportunity knocked. I turned slightly toward my left and "stroked" my flag right between Coach Jones's legs without him seeing it. This may have been the most perfect flag I had ever thrown. While those two were still making eye contact, the referee motioned him back toward the sideline. Jones had put his hands on his hips at this point. Out of frustration, he looked down toward the ground before walking away. As he looked down, he noticed for the first time that there was a penalty flag perfectly placed between both of his feet. He knew immediately that it was his fault a foul had been called.

As he stood there, he dropped his shoulders and slumped like all the air had been let out of his body. He wasn't mad at me. I think he knew the end was near.

Each time I saw Butch over the next three years, he always made it a point to come and say hello to me. We never talked about that foul in Knoxville.

WHAT DO YOU THINK?

On January 2, 2006, the Fiesta Bowl was played between the Buckeyes of Ohio State and the Fighting Irish of Notre Dame. Ohio State led at halftime, 21–7. It was never a close game.

Ohio State was the designated home team. Since that left Notre Dame as the visitor, I had them on my sideline.

Early in the game, an Ohio State offensive lineman absolutely demolished the right defensive tackle for the Irish. It was what is referred to as a "pancake block." Charlie Weis immediately started yelling that he had been held. I thought to myself that the only holding going on was this defensive player trying to hold on for his life. Wilbur Hackett, a great official, was the umpire in this game. Wilbur, a University of Kentucky alum, was also one of the first Black football players to break the color barrier in the Southeastern Conference.

Shortly after the previously mentioned play, we had a TV break. I was standing with Wilbur and mentioned Weis's tirade, that he wanted a holding foul. Wilbur simply looked at me and said, "Hell no!"

Just before the half, Notre Dame intercepted the ball in midfield around the fifty-yard line and the ball was returned for a touchdown. Or so we thought. Just after the score, Al Ford, our replay official, hit the pagers and notified us that he was going to review the play. In unison, we shut down the game for him to look at the action surrounding the interception.

In a situation like this, the line judge and head linesman go to the sidelines and stand near the coaches. If there are any questions or options that could result from the replay decision, these need to be explained to the coaches. In this case, Al was simply looking to see if the ball had been caught cleanly and to make sure he hadn't touched the ground, nullifying the touchdown.

After I had explained what was being reviewed, Coach Weis and I were standing in the coaching area just waiting for the review to finish. Just then, Weis asks, "What do you think?"

I replied, "I don't know, but they'll make sure it's right." I didn't have the luxury of looking at the play from multiple angles while in slow motion.

"No, that's not what I mean. Do you think I should go for two if the touchdown stands?"

I forced myself not to look at him. I didn't want my body language to reflect what my mind was thinking: *Are you f**king serious? Here you are being paid millions of dollars to make those kinds of decisions and you want me to make it for you?*

I mentally recalled working the Georgia-Clemson game in October of 1991. Clemson was ranked number six in the country. Georgia won, 27–12. Vince Dooley was coaching Georgia and Ken Hatfield was the head man for the Tigers. The Bulldogs grabbed the momentum early in the game and for most of the first half.

Clemson scored a touchdown with 4:29 remaining in the fourth quarter. The Tigers were showing some life after trailing for the entire game. Coach Hatfield decided to go for two and cut the lead to six. His team would still need a touchdown to win. At this point, a two-point conversion might have been too early.

Georgia denied Clemson's two-point attempt. As the Tigers were leaving the field, their heads were down, and their enthusiasm was deflated. This game was over right then and there.

Going back to Coach Weis's question, I simply responded,

"How's your team going to react if they don't make it?" I walked away.

As it turns out, the touchdown was taken off the board, and the ball was returned to the spot of the interception. The defender had, indeed, touched the ground with his knee right after the catch.

Mike "Square Head" Taylor was the line judge in the game. He really beat himself up for not being able to make the ruling on this play. It pained him for the ruling to be made from the press box.

After the game, I consoled him with a cooler of beer while we soaked in the salt water hot tub outside of our hotel rooms. Scottsdale, Arizona, was a nice place to visit in January.

YOU GOT
TO HELP US

In November of 2010, the University of Tennessee-Chattanooga played at Auburn. Cam Newton was guiding the offense for the Tigers. This game was over during the warm-up period prior to the game. The Auburn captains for the coin toss were twice as big as those for the Moccasins.

Newton played with Chattanooga's defense like a man among boys. Auburn started playing their second- and third-string guys in the second quarter.

I had UT-Chattanooga on my sideline. The whining and crying from the coaches and players were the worst I had ever experienced, except perhaps those from Ball State. Every play resulted in complaints about holding, facemasks, late hits, pass interference, clipping, etc. You name it, I heard it. All I wanted to do was get the game over with.

The Moccasins committed a holding foul while trying to slow down Auburn's defensive lineman. After we administered the penalty, I headed back to the sideline to set up the chains. I was met by the same whines and cries as before. However, this time, Coach Russ Huesman was yelling, "Come on, Gus, you've got to help us out!"

Out of frustration, I replied, "Coach, I'm helping all I can, but I need a little more effort out of you and your guys!"

Final score: Auburn, 62; UT-Chattanooga, 24.

I expected a call from the conference office on Monday to reprimand me for my comment. Fortunately, it never came.

The only thing Tennessee-Chattanooga beat that day was the spread.

THEY'RE FIGHTIN'

In 1997, Ole Miss played Mississippi State in Starkville, Mississippi, on Thanksgiving Day. It's known as the Egg Bowl. For some strange reason, I decided to drive over to the game that morning, leaving home around three a.m. I was taking a huge chance, but luckily, I made it without any problems. Plus, I had the added benefit of extra-light traffic. Nobody is on the roads that early on Thanksgiving Day. I pulled into the hotel parking lot at eight o'clock sharp.

Because it was the last regular game of the season, our pregame meeting was going to be brief. We had already had a full season's worth of preparation. Our meeting started around 9:30 and lasted about thirty minutes. I dressed in Eddie Powers and Gerald Hodges's room. The crew left for the stadium at 10:45, in plenty of time for our one p.m. kickoff.

Thanksgiving is historically a day to praise and thank God for blessings He bestows on us and to ask Him to heal the nation's wounds. It's a day for brotherly love. Such was not the case in Starkville this day.

It's hard to drag people to a football game on Thanksgiving Day. It's even harder when the weather is damp and cold. Mississippi's hunting season adds another excuse for those that might attend the game. Considering all these distractions, the crowds at the Egg Bowl are always large. The game between Ole Miss and State is one of the most intense rivalries in the country. These people hate each other. Even on Thanksgiving Day.

Once at the stadium, we went to our locker room. Mississippi State did not have the best accommodations in the conference, but it was at least warm and dry. Mike New and Eddie Powers checked each team's game balls while the referee, Doyle Jackson, and umpire, Ted "Dr. Dog" Davis, went to meet with the head coaches. Jackie Sherrill coached State and Tommy Tuberville was the head man at Ole Miss.

As is always the case, at least two officials go out onto the field during warm-ups sixty minutes prior to kickoff. On this day, Mike New and Eddie Powers drew the short straws to monitor the players who go out early. I had already settled into a corner of our locker room. With a pile of towels for a pillow, I managed to get in a short nap before the game.

Suddenly, I was awakened from a deep sleep. Eddie threw the door open and yelled, "They're fightin'!" We all got up and hustled out of our locker room. We trotted down the hall and out of the double doors leading out to the ramp going to the field. As we cleared the maroon-and-white awning that the players walk through, the field became visible.

Fighting was an understatement.

We entered the field area from the south endzone. Mississippi State's team area was to our left and Ole Miss's was on the right. There were players everywhere in between, throwing punches, pushing, shoving, and kicking each other. If you want to get a sense of what it looked like, do an online search and enter "1997 Egg Bowl Fight."

Ted Davis and I were the last two out of the tunnel leading to the field. When we reached the goal post, he stopped. I asked him what he thought we should do. He replied, "I'm not doing anything and you're not going out there." There was nothing we could do, except get hurt. So, we just took out our game cards and started recording the number of the most egregious players in the melee. It didn't take but a few moments and we both had a long list of numbers.

Mississippi State had a prized recruit at the game, and he

even decided to throw himself into the middle of the bedlam. After taking a fist or helmet to the face, he was escorted off the field toward where Ted and I were standing. As he got closer, you could see his face was a bloody mess. Dr. Dog calmly said, "State will have to give him a full ride now." Maybe they did.

No one really knows exactly how it all started but I do know who the main instigators were. Eddie Gran was coaching wide receivers for Ole Miss and Melvin Smith was coaching defensive backs for Mississippi State. Melvin and I were teammates at Millsaps College. Eddie and I had gotten to know each other during the SEC coaches and officials golf tournament. At some point during warm-ups, one group of players was encouraged to interfere with the other. Not wanting to give up any ground, a stand was made.

After some twenty minutes of mayhem, there were enough state troopers and local law enforcement on the field to get the fight under control. They numbered well over one hundred in personnel. Eventually, both teams were sent to their respective locker rooms.

As officials, we didn't really know what to do. Fortunately, Doyle was contacted by an administrator on the Mississippi State staff. They took him to a telephone on the sideline which connected with the press box. When he picked it up, he was told by an SEC conference representative that the commissioner, Roy Kramer, would deal with this the following week. "Let 'em play." We were off the hook.

Both NCAA and SEC conference rules state that any player charged with fighting will be ejected from the game. If we had followed through with this to the letter, the game would not have been played that day.

Our crew gathered for one final meeting prior to kickoff. We agreed that we would eject any player immediately from the game if they resumed anything close to what we had witnessed during warm-ups. We had to keep this game under control at all costs.

Once the game got underway, it became one of the easiest games I had ever officiated. The players had gotten whatever it was out of their system before we got started. We didn't have any problems. Ole Miss prevailed, 15–14, over Mississippi State that day. The Rebels would take the Golden Egg trophy back to Oxford, where it would stay for the next 365 days.

31–0: THE BEST GAME I EVER WORKED

There are always the same two or three questions that come up whenever I'm asked to make a presentation or speech: Who's the worst coach you've ever seen? What's the best stadium in the league? What's the best game you've ever been in?

All coaches can be difficult to deal with, especially when they're getting their ass kicked.

Every stadium has its own unique personality. In alphabetical order, here are the things I think about when each SEC school is mentioned.

- Alabama: The Million Dollar Band playing "Yea, Alabama, Crimson Tide."
- Auburn: Flying one of their eagles around the stadium prior to the game.
- Arkansas: The crowd calling the Hogs . . . "Woo Pig Sooie."
- Florida: "Two Bits" cheer to start the game in the Swamp.
- Georgia: The bugle player in the top southwest corner of the stadium.
- Kentucky: The crowd singing "My Old Kentucky Home" during pregame.
- LSU: The Golden Band from Tiger Land and the Golden Girls.

- Ole Miss: "Hotty Toddy, by damn."
- Mississippi State: Cowbells.
- Missouri: Truman's Taxi.
- South Carolina: Playing "Sand Storm" before kickoff.
- Tennessee: Pride of the Southland Band forming the Power T for the team to run through.
- Texas A&M: "Yell Squad" and "The Twelfth Man."
- Vanderbilt: "Anchor Down."

The best game I was ever involved with occurred on January 2, 2016. San Antonio hosts the Alamo Bowl each year. It's usually played between a team from the Big 12 and one from the PAC 12. This game was a matchup between the University of Oregon and Texas Christian University.

Besides being two very good football teams, there were some background stories that made this game even more intriguing. Oregon finished the regular season with a record of 8–3, while TCU finished 10–2. The previous year, the Oregon Ducks had played in the CFP National Championship game, losing to Ohio State, 42–20. TCU had preseason Heisman–hopeful Trevone Boykin playing quarterback. For a mid-level bowl game, this had the ingredients to be a very exciting football game.

I arrived in San Antonio in the early evening of December 31, New Year's Eve. After checking into the hotel, I walked over and met the rest of the crew for dinner at a nearby Tex-Mex, restaurant, and it was very good.

After eating, we went back to the hotel and went up on the rooftop lounge area to watch the local fireworks. It was quite amazing. There were so many fireworks off in the distance that it appeared the whole city was shooting off all manner of displays.

Word was beginning to spread that there were some serious issues leading up to the game. Particularly when it came to TCU. These rumblings soon became reality.

Very early in the morning of December 30, 2015, apparently Trevone Boykin decided to forgo team rules, break curfew, and go into a downtown San Antonio bar, Pat O'Brian's. After scuffling with employees, the police were called. After striking a police officer, Boykin was arrested. Gary Patterson, the head coach of TCU, immediately suspended his starting quarterback and sent him back to Fort Worth.

Later that same morning, the coaching staff decided who was going to play quarterback for them in two days. Bram Kohlhausen was called into a meeting that began a series of events that would change his life.

Bram walked on at the University of Houston and worked with the team for two years. He was redshirted his freshman year and saw very limited action as a third-string quarterback his sophomore season. Over those two years, he only saw action in three games.

His junior year, he transferred to Los Angeles Harbor College. My understanding is that he suffered a season-ending shoulder injury early in the season. At the end of his one year at Los Angeles Harbor, he moved back to Houston, Texas.

Not wanting to give up on football, he was given the opportunity to walk on at Texas Christian University. During the 2014 and 2015 regular seasons, Bram again saw very limited action.

In his senior year of 2014, Bram played sparingly during four games. For the year, he was seven of nine in pass completions for a total of forty-three yards.

As a fifth-year senior, he saw a little more playing time. During the 2015 regular season, he was able to complete twenty-seven of forty-three passes, for a total of 369 yards.

His mom and dad traveled to almost all his games. Even if

just to watch him sit on the bench or to play very limited time. His dad tried to make it to every game.

On the morning of December 30, Bram was named the starting quarterback for the first time in his NCAA Division I career. He was going to lead the Horned Frogs against the Ducks, who had played for the national championship the previous year.

Bram hadn't planned even being in the game and had misplaced his playbook. He had to get an extra copy from his position coach. He had about forty-eight hours to study it.

The game was scheduled to kick off on the evening of Saturday, January 2. It was the only game on television that night, so the national audience was large.

At the end of the first half, Oregon was ahead, 31–0. As officials, we were discussing how we were going to really need to have a presence on the field and not let things get out of hand.

When we walked back on the field from our locker room, we noticed a lot of fans had already left the Alamo Dome.

Right at the end of the first half, Oregon's starting quarterback took a big hit. When the second half got underway, a new quarterback was in for Oregon. Bram was still at the helm for TCU.

Very quickly, the momentum of the game began to change, and it was swinging in TCU's direction. At the end of the third quarter, the score was Oregon, 31–TCU, 17. Midway through the fourth quarter, TCU kicked a field goal and cut the lead to eleven points. With three and a half minutes remaining in the game, TCU scored a touchdown and successfully scored on a two-point try. They now only trailed by three points.

With time running out late in the fourth quarter, TCU kicked a field goal to tie the game at 31-all. Gary Patterson had changed shirts at halftime. He claims to have had his "smart" shirt on.

In the first overtime, both teams scored touchdowns and successfully kicked their extra point to again tie at 38-all. During the second overtime, each team was held to a field goal making the score 41-all.

In the third overtime period, TCU went on offense first. Three plays later, they were in the endzone for a touchdown. But they missed the two-point conversion. Because it was after two overtime periods, they had to go for two. Now it was Oregon's turn to go on offense.

Four plays from scrimmage were run by the Ducks for a total of two yards. TCU had held Oregon from scoring. TCU had scored on all nine of their final possessions of the game. It was the largest comeback in bowl history. All with a walk-on quarterback.

One of Bram's brothers was on the sideline during the game. After the final buzzer, his brother was able to secure another sideline pass from an Oregon fan for $100. He was able to get his mother down on the field to celebrate with her son. It was a bittersweet moment. Bram's father, Bill, had passed away the previous November. He never got to watch his son start a college game.

With his mother and brother at his side, Bram was designated the game's MVP.

When the second semester of his fifth year started a few days later, he was called in to Coach Patterson's office. In this meeting, Bram was awarded a full scholarship for the remainder of his time in college.

Rumor has it that Disney bought the rights to his story. If ever made into a movie, I don't know who I would want to play me. It really doesn't matter. I was a part of history. More importantly, I was a part of a story that is a textbook definition of perseverance. Thank you, Bram!

PUDDING FROM HEAD TO TOE

On October 26, 1996, Mississippi State traveled to Baton Rouge to take on LSU. Jefferson Pilot televised the game in their 11:30 a.m. central-time slot. It was the first game of the day. We experienced all kinds of weather during the game.

There was a steady rain which fell all day long on the Friday before. The field at Tiger Stadium was saturated. The crown on this field was steeper than any other in the league. As a wing official, you felt like you were running uphill every time you moved from the sideline to the middle of the field. If each line-of-scrimmage official was standing on their respective sideline, you could not see anything from about eight inches below the knees. Even with this crown to help with the drainage, the field held water.

At the beginning of the game, the grass on the field was in pretty decent shape. There were some very light rain showers. But during halftime, we had a major thunderstorm pass right over the stadium. We came out for the second-half kickoff—there was standing water everywhere. The sideline drainage area had four to six inches of standing water.

Late in the third quarter, the sun broke through and eventually, the clouds moved out for a beautiful, early afternoon. The field was still a mess. It even smelled bad because of the mixture of mud and fertilizer. When players ran or hit the ground, water plashed in all directions.

At one point, as LSU was driving toward the south endzone, there was a run right up the middle. Billy Becket, the back judge, was right in front of the runner as he was tackled on the mid-field logo. It wasn't much of a logo anymore. The players had turned it into something that resembled more of a Mardi Gras pudding.

When this play was ruled dead, Billy looked like he had yellow, purple, and white mud splashed all over the front of him, from head to toe. Al Ford, Butch Lambert Jr., and I looked at Billy almost in disbelief. How could you get that much mud on you? It would take a three-year-old having a temper tantrum to make him look like he did. I seriously doubt that his uniform was ever clean enough to wear again.

KEEPING THINGS IN PERSPECTIVE

On September 14, 2019, I was scheduled to work in the Arkansas State game at Georgia in Athens. These are basically "paycheck games" for these smaller schools. Yes, anything can happen on any Saturday, but not on this day.

This weekend had a very different feel. Blake Anderson, the head coach of Arkansas State, had decided to come back to coaching after taking several weeks off to mourn the loss of his wife, Wendy. Four weeks earlier, she had passed away after a two-year battle with cancer.

The outpouring of support from all the people from Georgia was unbelievable. There was a great sign of respect from the Georgia coaching staff and administration. The Georgia student section dressed in pink to show their respects.

Georgia won big, 55–0, but they did not run up the score. The whole afternoon was a tribute to Wendy and a show of respect and support for Blake.

Being on the sideline with a coach reveals much about their character. This day, he was there to coach his players and he did so admirably. Yes, it was solemn in the team area, but they were all united.

As the game was winding down, I had a chance to go and shake the coach's hand. I said nothing. There were no words. He looked me straight in the eyes as we were standing there. He was hurting inside but he appreciated my gesture. Toward the end of our encounter, he simply said, "Thank you."

The game was not important that day. It was a symbol of hope, strength, and dignity.

ALWAYS EXPECT THE UNEXPECTED WITH LES MILES

A tropical depression hovered over Baton Rouge when South Carolina played LSU in September of 2007. It rained from the time I got to the hotel on Friday afternoon and well after I left for home on Sunday.

The month of September always has a high probability of bad weather. It's hot and thunderstorms can cause many problems, from sloppy field conditions, travel issues, and weather delays of games. It's also hurricane season in the south.

This game was touted as the game of the week in the Southeastern Conference. Steve Spurrier was in his third season as the head coach of the number-twelve ranked Gamecocks. They had won their first three games of the season.

LSU was also undefeated and ranked number two nationally. The steady rain didn't deter the ninety-three-thousand-plus fans in attendance. It was a great atmosphere for a midafternoon showdown.

South Carolina scored first and very early in the ball game to take the lead, 7–0. LSU scored a minute and a half later to tie the game and then added another twenty-one unanswered points. The Gamecocks put nine points on the board in the fourth quarter before losing by a final score of 28–16.

South Carolina won their next three games. In mid-October,

the Gamecocks lost to Vanderbilt, which was the beginning of a five-game losing streak to close out the season and finish with a record of 6–6.

There were some memorable moments during the game. Near the end of the first half with 1:24 left on the game clock, LSU lined up for a thirty-two-yard field-goal attempt. In typical Les Miles form, they ran a fake and scored a touchdown on the play. They executed it so well that I was the only one on the field that could have made the tackle.

When the ball was snapped to the holder, he simply tossed it blindly over his shoulder to the kicker, #6, who ran around the right side of the formation. Coach Spurrier was pissed. He had been tricked by the "Mad Hatter."

The 2007 season also saw another rule change regarding interference with the opportunity to make a fair catch. Players catching punts are very vulnerable. To afford them protection, they cannot be touched until after they complete the catch.

The rule had been modified several times during the mid-2000s. Early contact never changed—it has always been a fifteen-yard penalty—what did change was the penalty for players being close to a receiver as he attempted to catch the ball. At one point, there was no foul, then five yards was added if a kicking team member was too close to the front of the receiver. Then the donut was added to the equation and no player could be within a yard of the receiver anywhere. In 2007, they changed the five-yard penalty to fifteen yards.

With fourth and nine on their own thirty-two-yard line, South Carolina was forced to punt. Jared Mitchell, for LSU, called for a fair catch on his forty-four-yard line. A flag came in for kick-catch interference against South Carolina. When it was announced that the penalty would be fifteen yards, Spurrier went ballistic. He started yelling at me that it's only a five-yard penalty. When he finally slowed down during his tirade, I explained that there had been a rule change during the previous offseason, changing all kick-catch interference fouls to a fifteen-yard penalty.

This further added to his outburst. He clearly didn't know this rule change and me having to correct him only made things worse. He responded by telling me, "Well, next time, I'm just going to have my players go down and wipe the receiver out!" He did this while shaking his visor right in front of my face. It was so close that water was spraying all over my face. Fortunately for him, we were backed up in the coaching area. Had this been on the field, he would have earned an unsportsmanlike conduct foul. From previous experience, I didn't want to go there.

When I finally got him to understand the rule change and the consequences of his suggested player reaction to this change, I calmly told him, "Please don't shake your visor in my face again."

On Monday morning, I got a call from the coordinator of the SEC football officials. He explained to me that Coach Spurrier had called him to complain about me—again. Instead of backing me up, I was told that I shouldn't talk to a coach like that. "Sure, whatever you say."

It would do no good to argue with the coordinator. He holds all the cards and holds your career in the palm of his hands. It's best to play along and agree with him. But I can promise one thing: had it happened again, I wouldn't make a request; I would have penalized him. I think Spurrier knew that, even though he would probably never admit it.

FLYING
CHICKEN BONES

My first big break in college officiating occurred during the 1990 season. There's a lot to unpack in this story.

Bill Goss, an SEC referee, and Dan Post, an ACC field judge, were assigning games for an association they created called the Collegiate Football Officials Association. This group of officials was made up of guys working in the SEC, ACC, and people like myself that were wanting to move up. The CFOA supplied officials for Western Kentucky, Samford University, Georgia Southwestern, Georgia Southern, and the University of Central Florida. Typically, crews were made up of veteran officials with no more than two up-and-comers, like me. It provided game experience where prospective officials could be seriously evaluated.

Bill called me on a Thursday morning and asked me could I work a game on Saturday. "Sure," I replied. You cannot say no to those that can have an impact on your future. He began to explain the assignment. "I need you to work in the Georgia Southern-Marshall game in Huntington, West Virginia, Saturday night. This is a big game. Marshall is ranked number one and Southern is ranked number two in Division I-AA."

"Okay," was my reply.

"I don't know how you're going to get there. We can only pay you two hundred dollars. Here are your crew members: Dan Post will be the referee; Ray Moon is the head linesman; James "Pud" Mosteller is the umpire; you'll work as the line judge; Eddie Powers is the side judge; Bill Bowdoin is the field judge; and Prince Pollard will be the back judge. I'll send you the hotel information so you can make your reservation. Do you have any questions?"

Yes, I had a shitload of questions, but opportunity knocked, and it was time to make the most of it. I knew right away that $200 wasn't going to cover my costs. I had a three-year-old and money was tight in our household. Questions or not, I needed to take this assignment.

Jim Donnan was the head coach at Marshall and Tim Stowers was the man at Georgia Southern. I would be working on the home-team sideline.

I called Bill Bowdoin Thursday evening and we decided to split the hotel room. I was able to get a cheap flight on Delta. The only other expense was money for food. I could hold that to a minimum.

Because it was a night game, I decided to risk it and fly up on the morning of the game. Plus, I had a high school game the night before. When flying directly into Huntington, you can still see the aftermath of the damage done by the plane carrying the Thundering Herd when it crashed on approach to the airport in November of 1970. Very chilling to this day.

I arrived at the hotel on Saturday around eleven a.m., just in time to meet up with some of the other officials for lunch. I didn't know these guys very well, but they took me in and treated me like I belonged there.

We drove ourselves to the stadium and parked in spots designated for the officials. I don't remember if we dressed at the hotel or the stadium. However, I can still visualize what the locker room looked like: a tiny air conditioner was mounted close to the ceiling in a cinder block wall, everything was white with eight or ten gray metal folding chairs and a table in the middle of the room.

This was to be the last home game in this particular stadium. Marshall was building a new one. ESPN scheduled our game in their prime-time slot on that Saturday evening. The place was electric.

The first half was uneventful. Marshall was ahead, 7–3, at the half. Georgia Southern took the lead in the third quarter, 10–7. With about six minutes left in the fourth quarter, Marshall scored and went up, 14–10. Then things got really interesting, especially for an unproven official like me. It was time to experience trial by fire.

Marshall's defense held tough against Georgia Southern on a second down. Time was running out for the Eagles. They had to get a first down to have a chance at driving down the field and winning the game. A field goal was of no use to them. They had to get the ball into the endzone.

Everyone in the stadium was on their feet. In situations like this, you want every play to come to you. Marshall's quarterback, Raymond Gross, took the third down snap, rolled to his right, and threw the ball into the flat right out in front of me. A Marshall player stepped in front of the receiver, intercepted the ball, and fell to the ground. I moved into the spot, killing the play, and pointing possession for Marshall.

The place was going wild. All Marshall must do was run out the clock. Then came the whistle.

Trailing the play from behind, Dan Post came running over to where Gross threw the ball from and ruled that his knee was down before the pass was thrown. Jim Donnan was now losing his mind behind me. He was yelling he wasn't down. We rushed a new ball into the umpire so we could get the game back in play as soon as possible. Southern would have the ball for one more chance to make a critical first down. Replay didn't exist back then.

There was a tradition at Marshall concerning chicken bones. It seems that when the situation called for it, fans who've brought fried chicken to the game to eat would throw chicken bones onto the field. This situation called for an aerial assault of chicken bones. A prolonged onslaught ensued.

Georgia Southern converted the fourth down, proceeded

on down the field, and scored the go-ahead touchdown with thirty seconds left on the clock. They led, 17–14.

Marshall couldn't do anything offensively after receiving the kickoff from Southern and the game clock ran out. We hastily retreated to our locker room.

People were banging on the door and yelling at us. We had to have local police come and dispel the crowd. After a long time waiting in the dressing room for the "all clear" signal, we went to the cars parked in the designated officials parking spots. Dan Post was taking a maiden voyage in his brand new, gold-colored Cadillac Sedan Deville. Someone had decided it was a good idea to key his car. They couldn't know which one of us owned it, but they knew it was an official's vehicle. The president at Marshall said he wasn't going to pay for it.

We watched the evening news back at the hotel in hopes that they would have some highlights from our game. Dan Post had missed the call, bad. The reruns on TV showed that Georgia Southern's quarterback was far from being down. Actually, by about six inches. There was nothing we could do to make the correction. We were sick. My chances of moving up were now in question.

The next morning, Dan offered to let me ride with him and his wife out of Huntington. Maybe he was looking for reinforcement. Anyway, instead of flying out of there and make a connection back to Atlanta, he would drive that first leg to the airport where said connection was supposed to take place. Airlines were a lot more flexible back then. Airlines would redeem competitors' paper tickets.

After being dropped off at the airport and saying good-bye, a sinking feeling developed in my stomach. It didn't seem like we had driven long enough compared to the flight I had taken the morning before. As it turned out, I was at the wrong airport; my ride was gone and there was no one to call. The lady at the ticket counter said I could take a chance and go standby on a flight to Atlanta which left in about an hour. I really needed to get back home. A chance was not in my playbook at that moment. I paid her about $125 for a confirmed seat on the flight.

I proceeded to the gate after stopping to get a bite to eat. They took my ticket and told me to go on out to the plane, an older DC3, one of the most reliable aircrafts on the planet. Coincidentally, I took my seat, next to "Pud," the umpire from the previous night's game. He asked why I didn't ride with him. He looked confused when I told him, "I got dropped off at the wrong airport!"

The engines started, blue-white smoke billowed out of the engines, and off we went to Atlanta.

The extra airline ticket blew my expenses well past my game fee of $200. The return flight was half full. I should have gone standby! My son was glad to see me when I got home, so it was worth it. My wife wasn't so sure.

GUYS, ARE Y'ALL GETTING THIS?

LSU played Florida, in Gainesville, on October 7, 2017, five days after the death of Tom Petty. LSU won the ball game, surviving a late rally by the Gators, 17–16.

At the end of the first quarter and third quarter, the field is flipped, and the teams switch ends. There's a lot that goes on during this break. The ball position, down, distance, time outs left, and other details are written down and confirmed among the crew. When play resumes, everything should be the same as it was at the end of the previous quarter, just going in the opposite direction.

During the quarter break of the second half, I had finished making sure the chains were reset properly. We were on the northern end of the playing field. Matt Loeffler, Stan Weihe, and Mike Shirey were standing on the thirty-five-yard line oblivious to what was going on in the stadium. Over the communication system we were using, I asked, "Guys, are y'all getting this?"

The crowd in the stadium had broken out in a Tom Petty tribute. Petty was a Gainesville native but never attended the University of Florida. He worked for the school as a groundskeeper for a while, then he became an international rock-and-roll icon.

I stood amazed at how the entire crowd was singing in unison. As we were coming out of the TV break, the song was still resonating over the field. They were still singing when the ball was snapped to start the fourth quarter.

To this day, it is a tradition in the Swamp for the crowd to sing "I Won't Back Down" during the second-half quarter break.

TOUCHDOWN, COCKY

Spring games are not real serious for most officials. It's an opportunity to get out and run around with your cohorts. It fills a void in people's lives. Fans need a "football fix" and the spring game provides. An official is almost relegated to that of being a ball chaser. Go get it, put it down, and do it all over again.

Because officials are prohibited from working games for schools they attended in college, the spring game gives them a chance to get back on campus and visit with former players and coaches. You normally try to work spring games that are close to home. Your compensation for officiating these games is a fraction of what you're paid to do the same for a regular-season game—$125. Oh, they will provide a little gas money—$0.55 per mile, one way. No airfare.

I worked South Carolina's spring game for several years. It was fairly well attended, maybe ten or fifteen thousand fans. When Lou Holtz was hired, the number of fans increased dramatically. The South Carolina faithful were expecting a resurrection. They almost got one. His record was not all that great, but he did reinvigorate the fan base.

In Y2K, I drove over to Columbia, South Carolina, for their spring game. I left home early on a Saturday morning. Because we dressed at the stadium, I parked right across the street from Williams-Brice. This was Holtz's second spring game, and the crowd was pretty juiced. The band was in their normal place in the stands. The weather was perfect.

There were more than enough officials to work the game. (That's usually the case.) You can count on having one or two potential officials who are there to officiate in hopes of making an impact on the conference office. Because there are so many extra guys, you can do one of three things: One, you can rotate out and watch from the sidelines. Two, you can work other positions on the field. And three, you can leave early and go home—or wherever else you may want to go.

The format of the game would go something like this: The first half would be run much like a regular game. Two fifteen-minute quarters, and the game clock was run according to the rules. The second half was much more relaxed. Generally, once each quarter started, the game clock kept running, even on incomplete passes. The only time it was stopped was under the direction of the head coach.

Spring practice is where the coaches evaluate the players. The spring game was more of a homecoming event. Let the players have some fun in front of the fans and pray someone doesn't get hurt.

In this game, I worked my primary position, the head linesman. However, I did switch out and work deep as side judge. In the fourth quarter, things had really gotten loose. For all intents and purposes, the scrimmage was over. It was just a formality to let the clock run out.

The second and third string was on the field, getting in a few reps. We were almost through when the quarterback dropped back to pass and threw a deep ball down my side-line, into the endzone. The South Carolina mascot, "Cocky," ran onto the field and caught the ball. Without any hesitation, I went up with a perfect touchdown signal. The crowd went wild. And no one got hurt!

OH, WHAT A SURPRISE

On October 7, 2000, I worked in the Georgia-Tennessee game in Athens. Tennessee had beaten Georgia nine straight times prior to this game. Jim Donnan was the head coach of the Bulldogs, and Phillip Fulmer was guiding the Volunteers.

Tennessee had a freshman quarterback by the name of Casey Clausen and Georgia's signal caller was Quincy Carter. The game was broadcast on ESPN with a seven o'clock kickoff.

I was a replacement on the crew working the game, led by referee Bill Goss. Their regular head linesman was Billy Schroer. Billy was a Georgia Tech graduate and he scratched Georgia from his list of schools he was eligible to work for.

Since the game was in Athens, I drove over from home that morning. Cumming, Georgia, is just an hour-and-fifteen-minute drive away. Even though the game finished after ten o'clock, I was able to go back home that evening. Being able to sleep in your own bed after a game is nice, even if you don't get back home until 12:30 or one o'clock in the morning.

The game had a lot of pregame hype. Both teams were ranked in the top twenty-five, with Georgia at number nineteen and Tennessee at number twenty-one. Maybe this would be Georgia's chance to break the stranglehold the Volunteers had on Georgia for almost a decade.

From an officiating standpoint, it was not a difficult game to work. Both teams were very competitive and there was a lot to play for. There was not any controversy about any of the fouls that were called, and the number of calls were about average for a normal game. In other words, the officials did a good job of keeping a low profile.

Leading into the fourth quarter, Georgia was up 14–10 over the Volunteers. With just over thirteen minutes left in the final quarter, Musa Smith scored on a half-yard run for the Bulldogs. Sanford Stadium exploded immediately after the score. The Georgia faithful started to sense that this night might be where they finally beat Tennessee.

Georgia's extra-point kick was good, but Tennessee had called a time out just prior to the snap so we had what's referred to as a "do-over." As the teams were setting up for the second extra-point attempt, Richard Morales, our field judge, got hit in the head by the football that was thrown back out of the stands from the previous kick. He went down like he had been shot. The Georgia athletic trainers came out to check on Richard. It was more of him being stunned than really hurt so in a matter of minutes, he was back and ready to go.

It was in the last five minutes of the game where things got really interesting. The final minutes of the game were played on the east end of the field. The student section is in the northeast corner of the stadium. With an eleven-point lead over the Volunteers, and momentum in their favor, Georgia was beginning to feel that a win was within their grasp.

The noise in the stadium was deafening. Tennessee hadn't quit, by any means, but they just couldn't execute the big play against Georgia coming down the stretch. Fans, led by the student section, began to stream out of the stands and down to the area just outside the famed hedges.

At 3:20 left in the fourth quarter, Tennessee had the ball on the Georgia four-yard line, fourth and one for a first down. Georgia held and, for all intents and purposes, the game was over.

Fans were starting to come through the gates and surrounded the east end of the field. More and more showed up.

It was really getting crowded. We had no room on the side-lines to work. At one point during a time out, we briefly dis-cussed switching ends of the field to finish the game. Ultimately, we didn't have to.

During a break in the action, I was standing around the bottom of the numbers that are painted on the field. I'm just running through some details that may be important as we finish the last few minutes of the game, like team time outs left, etc. Suddenly, I have something come flying by my head and bounce off the field in front of me. It's a two-liter bottle of Mountain Dew. Or that's what it appeared to be. I took a couple of steps forward, reached down, and pitched it back-ward toward the sideline. My right hand now had this sticky film all over it. I thought to myself, *Mountain Dew isn't this sticky!* I took a slight smell of my hand and realized it was what's referred to as "Kamikaze" mix. My next thought was, *They won't even remember having thrown that tomorrow morning when they wake up!*

Georgia had the ball, first and ten from their own four-yard line. Tennessee prevented the Bulldogs from getting a first down and Georgia was forced to punt. The clock was running down and Tennessee didn't have any time outs remaining. Students and fans were now really rushing the sidelines. We had people right up to the sidelines. Coach Donnan was pleading with the fans to not come on the field. Security was overwhelmed.

Getting the officials safely off the field after the game was now a big concern. We were all aware of how serious the situation was. Students were climbing over the hedges. It looked like a waterfall of people coming down from the stands.

We had to move the chains up to the sideline, six feet from the point where we normally place them. While I am standing close to the chain crew, I get a tap on the shoulder. Turning around, I lay eyes on the largest Georgia state trooper I have ever seen. He resembled the Russian Boxer Ivan Drago that Rocky Balboa fought in *Rocky IV*.

He tells me, "When this game is over, you come straight to me, you understand?"

"Yes, sir!"

The clock finally hits zero and all hell breaks loose. I start running from about the center of the field. Fans are everywhere. My whistle lanyard got caught in a guy's arm and momentarily stopped me. I was able to get it off from around my neck and I kept going. Two people stepped right in front of me. I dropped my shoulder and down went one of them. I hoped they were okay, but I had to get out of there. I found "Ivan" and grabbed the back of his gun holster while he led me off the field.

At around the fifteen-yard line, I looked over my left shoulder at the students who were rushing the field. When they hit the hedges, they were in for a big freakin' surprise. Instead of just running through them, they encountered the chain-link fence hidden within. Some students were stopped dead in their tracks and smashed up against the fence. There were some areas where the fence had been pushed over.

Once the officials were off the field and underneath the stadium, we made our way to the awaiting van. Everyone hopped in and we were off. Because of the game's excitement, most of the fans were still inside the stadium. There weren't many people in the surrounding area.

Once we cleared the stadium area and started making our way toward the Ramada Inn, where you could find the Frog Pond lounge, there was a collective sigh of "holy shit!" from all the officials. Wow, what an ending.

SOMETIMES, YOU'RE THE BALL

From an officiating standpoint, the 2004 Florida at Tennessee game was a mess. Both teams were highly ranked. This was a big game for the third weekend of September.

Neyland Stadium was packed. The crowd was fully behind the Volunteers. Florida led at the half, 21–14. The third quarter was played without either team scoring. Then, the fourth quarter happened.

Tennessee tied the game early in the quarter, 21-all. This game had all the makings of being a classic for the record books. Florida answered to retake the lead, 28–21, with eight minutes remaining. With about four minutes left, Tennessee scores to make it 27–28. They miss the extra point. You could feel the air escape from the crowd.

After the Vols kicked off, Florida's offense struggled. With a little over a minute to play, Florida had a third-and-three situation. If they make the first down, this game is over. The Gators ran it up the middle but were sacked for a one-yard loss. Then the shit hit the fan.

After the play, the side judge had a flag down for a dead ball, personal foul against Florida. In hindsight, it should have been offsetting dead-ball fouls. Instead of Florida punting from their thirty-seven-yard line, the fifteen-yard penalty backed them up to the twenty-two. The Neyland Stadium crowd erupted. This had a big impact on field position.

Florida was forced to punt. Tennessee took over on offense from their thirty-nine-yard line. Six plays later, James Wilhoit hit a fifty-yard field goal to put the Vols up, 30–28. He had redeemed himself for the missed extra point after their last touchdown.

Tennessee kicked off with six seconds left on the game clock. Florida ran one desperation play to end the game.

The next morning, I'm loading my car to go home, and I run into a couple of crewmates in the lobby of the hotel. They had a look about them that was not good. *Did something happen back at home?* I had that kind of feeling. I asked them what was wrong. They began to explain the situation. We're screwed.

It all started with the dead-ball foul that occurred late in the game. The previous play had been a running play that ended inbounds. After the penalty, Florida lined up to punt and the referee marked the ball ready for play. He should have also started the game clock but didn't. As a result, Florida didn't have the opportunity to run twenty-five additional seconds off the clock prior to punting the ball to Tennessee. Essentially, Tennessee was unfairly given that extra time during their succeeding possession. Did it affect the outcome of the game? Probably, but we'll never know for sure.

There was no way to spin this, as hard as some tried. I was told a letter of apology was going to be sent to Florida on behalf of the crew. Upon hearing this, I was adamant in replying, "Hell no, but if you do, keep my [expletive] name off of it." There would have been hell to pay.

We took an ass whooping from the media. Rightfully so. We were suspended for a game and switched out of the Florida-Florida State game to end the season. Finally, we were not considered when bowl assignments came out. Our last regular season game was back in Knoxville with their annual rivalry game against Vandy. The pregame meeting was a train wreck. It's a wonder we were able to complete the game as well as we did.

A few weeks after the Florida fiasco, we had a game at

Kentucky. Over the weeks in between, a particular song by Dire Straits kept creeping into the back of my mind. The title of the song is "The Bug." Essentially, it describes how, as you go through life, you'll have setbacks as well as success. A couple of the verses suggest that sometimes you're the windshield and other times the bug. Another verse describes sometimes being a Louisville Slugger while other times being the ball. At this point in the season, we were the ball.

Prior to the game in Kentucky, I made a call to the Louisville Slugger factory. I had seven bats custom made for the officials that had worked that Florida-Tennessee game. Each bat had the official's name, their field position, "Florida at Tennessee," and the date of said game.

During our pregame, we went around the room giving each official an opportunity to express their feelings. I asked to be the last to go. When it was my turn, I told them about this song I had been hearing by Dire Straits. After explaining the meaning of the song to them, I got up and pulled a box out from under the table. I then handed out the bats to each official. I concluded my remarks by telling my crewmates that we had been the ball long enough. It was now time to be the bat.

It is no fun being the ball, trust me.

WE'RE GOING TO ONSIDE KICK

On September 17, 1994, NE Louisiana played Georgia in Athens. The Indians won the coin toss and elected to defer their choice to the second half. Every official writes down the details of the coin toss on their game card to eliminate any possibility of confusion later in the game.

During this time in my career, the head linesman was positioned on what is referred to as the kicking team's restraining line for kickoffs. In other words, we lined up on the line where the ball is teed up.

When we were lined up and ready to have the opening kickoff, Ed Zaunbrecher, NE Louisiana's head coach, stepped in behind me and said, "We're going to onside kick." That's helpful information. Officials are taught to always look out for these types of situations but seldom are you told that it is actually going to happen.

The opening kickoff is an exciting time of the game. Everybody is focused on this play, and I mean everybody. The band is playing, the crowd is yelling, the players are jumping around on the sidelines. It's pandemonium. As always, I'm opposite the press box and NE Louisiana will be kicking from my right to left.

The kicker for NE Louisiana approaches the ball as his players begin running downfield. I'm ready and the only official who knows what's getting ready to happen. Just as he gets to the ball, his foot hits the very top of it and they are about to pull off a successful onside kick. The ball goes eleven yards, making the kicking team eligible to recover and maintain possession. The Indians fall on it. The closest Georgia players are twenty yards down field. They were retreating to set up the return.

This was one of those few opportunities where I was really going to be able to demonstrate what a badass SEC official I was. I move down the sideline to where they recovered the ball. I make a ninety-degree cut to square in running toward the dead ball. After killing the play by waving my arms over my head, I then pointed to which team had possession by extending my right arm. I'm poised like Adonis in the presence of eighty-five thousand spectators.

I see Len Harrington frantically running toward me from the other side of the field. *He wants a closer look to see how great a job I just did*, I was thinking to myself.

His first words to me are "What the hell are you doing?"

I replied, "It's NE Louisiana's ball!"

He followed up with, "If that's the case, you might want to point the other way!" I simply dropped my right arm and raised my left arm, like nothing ever happened. The game was on.

During our postgame debriefing, the observer for the game, Ed Dudley, entered the room, threw his notebook on the bed, looked me square in the eyes, and said, "Gus, that was the worst call I've ever seen, and Larry Munson agrees with me!"

Georgia won the game, 70–6. The next year, I won my first SECFOA Golden Whistle Award.

WE'RE GOING TO RUN THAT PLAY ALL NIGHT

On September 7, 1996, the University of Houston played LSU in Baton Rouge. On the third play of the game, I took the first big hit of my SEC-officiating career. The Cougars ran an inside trap for a gain of a couple yards. Nothing unusual, kind of routine. The mechanics we used at that time had us working very close to the players before and during the play. As I closed in to mark the spot of the runner being down, #55 for LSU made his introduction.

At the end of the play, Mr. Chuck Wiley and his 274-pound body launched over the top of the pile of players to avoid a late hit. As a result, his helmet hit me square in the chest as I was moving toward him. You may have heard the question, "What happens when an unstoppable force meets an immovable object?" I have firsthand knowledge of the answer to this paradox.

The first thing to hit the ground was the back of my head. Being young and resilient, I bounced up and acted like I was unfazed. I retrieved my hat, whistle, game card, pencil, bean bag, and pride from the ground around the scene of the accident. Coach Kim Helton was kind enough to inform me that they would be running that play often during the rest of the game. I thanked him for that helpful information, as I struggled to catch my breath.

Billy Beckett told me after the game that I looked like Wile E. Coyote from *Road Runner* after a cliff fall. It was actually a very fitting resemblance to what happened. Later that evening, Billy took me and my three broken ribs out to a local watering hole. The B&B's, along with the Coors Lights, kept the pain at bay until the wee hours of the morning.

I woke up to excruciating pain and had to slide out of bed. After getting dressed and packing my gear for the trip home, I headed to the Baton Rouge airport. Every move I made was carefully planned and executed to minimize the hurt. We eventually boarded the plane and taxied out for takeoff.

Immediately following the previous night's pregame national anthem, the Blue Angels did a flyover. As we were awaiting clearance for our departure back to Atlanta, the pilot came over the intercom system and informed us that if we looked out the left side of the aircraft, we could watch as this squadron of fighter jets departed for their home base in Pensacola. It was a spine-tingling experience.

The pilot of our jet was either a former fighter pilot or a "wannabe who never was"! Our takeoff was the most powerful I had ever endured. As the g-force pressed me hard into my seat, my broken ribs reminded me to always be aware of the inside-trap play.

MY LAST HURRAH!

The 2020 season was far from being a normal year. COVID-19 had changed the landscape of college football. Games were postponed and canceled throughout the season. Officials would test positive and be pulled from assignments. The restrictions on officials were many. Everything that once was considered normal was turned upside down.

Officials couldn't travel or room together. We were prohibited from going to restaurants for dinner. Pregame and postgame meetings were expected to be conducted via Zoom or some other internet meeting platform. Essentially, we were supposed to be in the same extended bubble as the players and coaches throughout the league.

My crew had three games impacted by COVID. Two were rescheduled and one was canceled. We were scheduled to work the Vanderbilt versus Georgia game in Athens. I drove over early on Friday afternoon so that I could meet a friend of mine for lunch. At this point of the season, I had pretty much had it with all the restrictions being placed on me, and a lunch was in order.

Prior to our food being brought out, I checked my phone one last time before I put it away while we ate. When I glanced at the screen, there were approximately a dozen text messages. The first one was from our referee, Matt Loeffler. Basically, it was saying, "Stand by, guys, there might be a problem with Vanderbilt and too many players testing positive with COVID." As I proceeded down the list of messages, I got to the one informing me that the game had been postponed. "Don't go to Athens."

My lunch date asked me what the matter was.

I told her, "There's not going to be a game tomorrow." It wasn't public knowledge yet, so I asked her to keep it to herself.

"No problem," she replied.

During this particular weekend, one of our crew members had a bad experience. Jesse Dupuy was already at the airport in Houston, Texas, when the previously mentioned text thread started. He had actually gone through the boarding process while getting the texts over about a thirty-minute period. He was part of the text thread and at one point, prior to the final decision being made to postpone the game, asked, "Should I get off the plane?" When he finally got confirmation that, in fact, the game was postponed, the plane doors had been closed. He was not getting off. Jesse had to fly to Atlanta, deplane, purchase a return ticket, and fly back to Houston. What a crappy way to spend a Friday afternoon. At least his son and daughter-in-law lived there, and he could spend time with them. Because this game was canceled inside the seventy-two-hour window prior to kickoff, we were paid our game fee.

The Vanderbilt versus Georgia game was eventually canceled altogether. One of our other games that got postponed was the Ole Miss versus LSU game in Baton Rouge. This game, however, was made up during the last weekend of the season. In fact, it was played on the same day as the SEC Championship game in Atlanta. For twelve teams, there was no prospect of playing for the conference championship.

Since this was the case, all that was at stake was the level of bowl game a team might be playing for. Some teams were playing only to stay out of last place.

I decided to fly into New Orleans and stay with my son and daughter-in-law. I flew in on a Friday morning and my daughter, Susan, picked me up at the airport. She let me borrow her car for the drive up to Baton Rouge. After dropping her at the apartment she had close to the hospital where she worked, I headed northwest. It rained most of the way to Baton Rouge. In fact, it rained all night and most of the next day.

I checked in to my room and went to grab a quick bite to eat before our Friday-night film session. We had a few substitutions on our crew due to conflicts and previous obligations by other crew members. We were without our normal referee, and we spent a little extra time going over details in case we needed to make changes on how we would perform certain things.

Our game was scheduled for a late afternoon kickoff. My plan was to drive back to New Orleans after the game and watch the second half of the SEC Championship game there. Since this was the case, I checked out of my room early and moved my stuff into Mike Shirey's room. I would dress there before the game and shower after the game.

The whole atmosphere was different than what you normally experience at LSU. The stadium was about a quarter of the way filled with fans. Social distancing was in place. With the weather the way it was, it probably wouldn't have been at capacity crowd anyway.

It ended up being a pretty good ball game. The field conditions were terrible. Even with all the drainage technology in place, the field became a muddy mess. Footing was getting really bad. You had to watch your step.

With about nine minutes to go in the game, Ole Miss was well inside LSU's ten-yard line and trying to score. They had driven the ball seventy-eight yards down the field.

Matt Corral goes under center, the ball is snapped, and he fakes a handoff to the tail back who dives up the middle. Corral then drops back with me thinking he is going to pass. I've got my eyes on two offensive linemen who are way downfield in the endzone. If the quarterback throws the ball, I got a foul for lineman downfield.

When I look back to get my eyes on the quarterback, he

has put the ball on his outside hip and is coming my way. I had moved out on the field about three or four yards and knew immediately that I was in trouble. All I could do was brace for impact. Corral and I collided just inside the goal line. All I saw was stars. His helmet hit me on the right side of my head. I went down. I wasn't completely out but I was certainly dazed.

While I was lying on my back, I looked straight up into the black sky. Big, cold raindrops were falling down on me. When the rain hit the stadium lights, it was like something out of *Star Wars*. It was actually pretty cool to look at.

Trainers were at my side quickly. I got up and staggered while trying to keep my balance. Blood was running down the side of my face. Immediately, someone had applied pressure to my head to help stop the bleeding. I figured I was done for the night. Probably done for my career. This was the second head shot I had taken in seven years.

Matt Corral was there making sure I was okay and apologizing for running into me. I told him it was my fault; I was out of position. Once he knew I was going to be okay, in spite of all the blood, he patted me on the chest and said, "You're one tough son of a bitch."

"No, you won this one," I replied. The crew made some adjustments and the alternate official moved to my positions.

The LSU training staff walked me off the field and to their training room. A doctor was waiting on me. After he cleaned the wound and he got a chance to see the damage, he asked me, "Stitches or glue?"

"Glue, doctor."

Once he got me glued up and bandaged, I headed back out to the field. There had been a very long review of a play and there was still a little over five minutes left on the game clock. I went back in and officiated the remainder of the game.

When we got back to the hotel, Mike let me shower first so I could get on the road to New Orleans as quickly as possible.

When I got out of the shower, he was on the phone. I figured he was talking to his wife, as he normally did after a game. It turned out not to be his wife—it was our coordinator of football officials.

At one point during the conversation, Mike said, "He's right here," obviously referring to me. Our coordinator never asked to speak with me to see how I was doing. Not that evening, not ever. He also told Mike that he needed to get a uniform shirt to work as a head linesman in an upcoming bowl game. Mike was normally a line judge.

Some bowl assignments had already been made. Mike was going to be an alternate in a game the following week or so. By moving him onto the field, I knew changes had been made. I was also realistic enough to know that our coordinator was going to keep me out of a bowl game because of the embarrassment he felt as a result of me being hit earlier that evening during our game.

Without Mike asking, I handed him my uniform shirt so he would have the proper letter when he worked out of his normal position as a head linesman. I held no ill feelings and haven't to this day.

When I was all cleaned up and dressed, I took off for New Orleans. It was now a steady downpour. I got to my son's house during halftime of the SEC Championship game. We had a couple of drinks and watched the rest of the game. The bottle of scotch he had for us that night was a really good single malt.

The next morning, plans had been put in place for having breakfast at this nice little cozy restaurant. Since I would be going straight to the airport from there, I showered, dressed, and packed all my gear for the flight back home. I made up my bed but handed the bloodied pillowcase to Brooke in hopes that the stains would wash out. She had work to do so my son, August, and I went to the restaurant, where we would meet up with Susan.

We had to wait about thirty minutes for a table. A very good Bloody Mary helped pass the time. Our name was called, and we were seated at a table in the middle of the restaurant. I wasn't sure if people recognized me as the official that was hit during the game from the night before, but several people were staring at me. It didn't matter. My children and I were having a great time together.

Chicken and waffles were my choice that morning. It was delicious. They each had their normal menu item. I decided to have another Bloody Mary.

After we finished breakfast, I said good-bye to Susan and August drove me to the airport. It was a different ride but, at the time, I couldn't explain it. He dropped me off at the curb with plenty of time to catch my flight. There was no feeling like I was in a rush. I told August, "Good-bye, I love you," and turned, walking into the terminal.

As I waited for my flight, which was delayed by about thirty minutes, I reflected back on the previous night's game. I thought about how I was in the wrong spot. I remembered what Matt Corral had told me. I was thankful for how the medical staff at LSU had taken care of me. I thought about giving my shirt to Mike. I think all of this, along with some other issues that had caused the ride to the airport to feel different. I sensed that I may have worked my last game but decided to put that aside.

In reality, it was a God thing. I was being provided comfort after a long career as a football official. As it turned out, I had worked my last game. Ole Miss at LSU on December 19, 2020, was my last hurrah.

Partners in Game Time

I'M THE MOST RELAXED PERSON HERE

The weekend of October 31, 1999, was the date of the World's Largest Outdoor Cocktail Party held annually in Jacksonville, Florida. This was my second of a total of five Florida-Georgia games. If you're a true football fan and have never been, put this on your bucket list.

I arrived in Jacksonville on Friday evening before the game. I had my fiancée with me, and we had driven up from Ft. Lauderdale, Florida. As we were unloading the car, we had a chance to visit with the line judge on the crew.

The kickoff time was 3:30 p.m. and this keeps things from feeling like you're having to hurry. We had breakfast at the hotel and then went into our pregame meeting. Doyle Jackson was our referee. This crew had been together for two years and worked very well as a unit. After our pregame meeting, Doyle asked me to hang around, as he had something he wanted to talk with me about.

"Sure, no problem. What's up?"

Doyle started the conversation getting right to the point. "Gus, Commissioner Kramer and Bobby [the SEC supervisor of officials] wanted me to talk with you about being on Coach Spurrier's sideline this afternoon. How are you feeling about it?"

I didn't laugh out loud, but I did to myself. I completely understood the reasoning behind them using Doyle as a liaison. I assured him that everything was going to be fine, as far as I was concerned. I even filled him in on some details leading up to my arrival in Jacksonville.

The conference's concerns arose from the last game I officiated between Florida and LSU the previous year. It was a huge game. Florida had been ranked number one in the nation and LSU beat them, 28–21. How the Tigers won the game was not reflected in the score. They physically outplayed Florida for much of the game.

During the game in Baton Rouge, I ended up penalizing Coach Spurrier for unsportsmanlike conduct. It ended up being a really big deal. Spurrier still hates my guts to this day. I was right, he was wrong.

I began by reminding Doyle that we were off the previous weekend. Knowing this, Cheryl, my fiancée, and I scheduled a vacation out to the Bahamas. We rented a very nice house on a two-and-a-half-acre island. It was three miles across the bay from Harbour Island on the northern end of Eleuthera. For seven days, the only inhabitants of this little island were just the two of us.

I finished telling Doyle what all had gone on over the past week and concluded it by saying, "I'm the most relaxed guy here." Doyle smiled and told me he wasn't concerned about things anyway. He was just the messenger. After hearing my story, he absolutely wasn't concerned.

We dressed, were taken to the stadium, and worked a very good ball game. I could have cared less about Coach Spurrier that day. His body language signaled he didn't like me and that was okay. Because he knew what I would do, he stayed out of my way and didn't say a word to me all game. Or maybe because he enjoyed beating Georgia so much and was busy calling ball plays, he didn't have time for me. Florida beat Georgia bad, 38–7.

My fiancée and I flew home after the game. The airport was not busy at all. It was close to midnight by the time we got our luggage. We were going to catch a cab for the trip from the Atlanta airport to Sandy Springs where I had left my car. Fortunately, we struck up a conversation with a limousine driver and he said he would be glad to take us there. He lived in Sandy Springs, and he was getting ready to go home anyway.

We chatted during most of the forty-five-minute ride. He asked where we had been. He was fascinated with what all we had done. He was a football guy—a Georgia fan. We talked about the game earlier that afternoon. He took the loss without complaining. He didn't hold back when he described how much he despised Coach Spurrier.

He started talking about the Florida game at LSU the previous year. He said the highlight of the game was Spurrier getting penalized. My fiancée smiled in the back seat. I didn't say anything.

When we got to where our car was parked, he helped unload the bags and put them in the trunk. Once he made sure the car would start, he came over to say good-bye. As I handed him the money for the trip, I told him, "I'm the guy that penalized Spurrier."

We talked for a few more minutes. It was time to get home. It made his day, for sure. He had met his football hero!

SOME ADULTS WILL ACT LIKE LITTLE KIDS

Ray Moon was one of the instrumental people that played an important role in my officiating career. It seemed like whenever I needed some support or encouragement, he was there. He was also one of the most literal and humorous people I knew. You couldn't figure out, at times, what he was going to do or say next.

Ray ran the SEC golf tournament for years. During my second year in the league, he recruited me to help him. Over the next several years, he groomed me to take over the event that was held in Montgomery, Alabama. I was glad to do it.

During the 1997 tournament, as Ray's assistant, I needed to be there on Thursday afternoon. We did some preliminary setting up and then a group of us went out to dinner. The Sahara restaurant on Edgemont Avenue was always one our first choices. The Sahara was a very nice restaurant with a private dining room that was made available to our group. They recognized us as regulars, even though it was only on an annual basis.

Ray and his wife, Luanne (a.k.a. "The Claw"), Jimmy Harper, Bob Patrick, Bob "Turkey" Lee, and Mike Wallace, along with his wife and two sons, made up the group. We had plenty of time to visit because the size of our group caused the service to be drawn out.

It was a little bit too long for Mike's sons. They got to the point where they started to fidget. In swooped Ray Moon to the rescue. He would entertain them and keep them from being bored.

The private room where we were seated was very well decorated. There were several expensive oil paintings on the wall of prominent individuals, including a former governor of Alabama, along with his wife, the First Lady.

Ray began to show the boys how to take small pieces of napkin and make spit balls. He demonstrated the proper size and how to add just enough saliva for the perfect projectile. The correct way to place it in a straw was explained and then, *woosh*, he showed how to blow it down range with good accuracy.

"Here, you try it!"

Over the next thirty minutes, periodic spit balls were shot by the boys. Whenever a behavior correction came from their parents or Luanne, Ray would assure them that they could continue what they were doing. Ray was enjoying it as much as they were.

Suddenly, there was chuckling from the boys and Ray. The vibe from the three of them was strange. It was then that the rest of the people at the table realized what had happened: the youngest son had executed the perfect shot!

Just below the right nostril on the First Lady's portrait was a big, white booger. Everyone at the table—except Ray, Josh, and Nathan—reacted the same way: "This isn't good. Maybe the owners and servers at the restaurant won't notice until after we leave." They didn't.

Ray and the boys were still celebrating and high-fiving as we left the restaurant. Some people will always be a kid at heart. And a troublemaker.

STOP TRYING
SO HARD

Around 2005, my very close friend, Skip Ramsey, drove me to Birmingham for the SEC preseason summer clinic. It was his first one, while hoping to get picked up and put on the roster of active officials.

The drive from Atlanta on Thursday and the meetings on Friday were uneventful. This would be a three-day ordeal that would conclude on Saturday, early afternoon. All the meetings were held in the large conference room of the SEC office and most of the officials stayed right across the street at the Ramada Inn.

Saturday was coordination day. The information talked about on Thursday and Friday was all brought together. It was designed to provide consistency between the officials throughout the season.

On Friday evening, just before turning in for the night, Skip and I made our plans for the next morning. We were going to get up early, shower, dress, and go ahead and pack our stuff in his van so that we could leave for home immediately after the meetings were over. We had it all figured out. Skip had taken the lead and he assured me that everything was under control, even the alarm clock. "Good night!"

When the alarm clock went off the next morning, I jumped up first and showered. While I was getting dressed, Skip followed suit and took over the bathroom. By the time he got dried off, I was dressed and packed, ready to go. As he walked into the room, I opened the door to go put my stuff in his van. Something was bad wrong.

It was very dark and quiet outside. I went on to the van and put my stuff in the back area. When I returned to the room, I asked Skip what time it was. He looked at the clock and said, "Six thirty."

In return, I replied, "No way."

My flip phone at that time didn't have a clock. But Skip's did. When he checked his, he looked at me and said, "I set the alarm clock wrong."

I then asked, "Well, what f**king time is it?"

"4:30."

He had set the clock on eastern time instead of central. "Well, what the hell are we going to do now?"

We decided to just drive around Birmingham for a while to kill some time. I'm sure a Dodge Ram van with tinted windows driving around downtown Birmingham in the dark early-morning hours didn't look like part of the illegal drug trade, but there we were. We only had to kill three and a half hours before our first meeting of the morning.

We drove all over the place, talking and listening to the radio. Suddenly, up ahead, we saw a beautiful sight. A sign illuminated that simply read, "HOT!" Skip immediately turned across two lanes of road and into the parking lot. We exited the parking lot with four dozen hot Krispy Kreme donuts. Who in the hell was going to eat four dozen donuts?

This first meeting started at eight a.m. sharp. Around 7:30, we walked into the conference office with three and a half-dozen donuts, though not really hot anymore. Within a few minutes, the boxes were empty.

At the conclusion of the meeting and some "best of luck" comments from Bobby Gaston, supervisor of officials, Skip and I started our trip back to Atlanta. First on the agenda, get gas. We had burned up about three quarters of a tank driving around earlier that morning. Second, get some beer.

We found a liquor store and went inside for beer. We struck up a friendly conversation with the guy running the place. In the end, we walked out with a case of beer, a cooler, and plenty of ice. The guy threw the cooler and ice in for free.

We settled in for the ride home and were passing the Birmingham airport when my phone rang. Another official was on the other end complaining about my presentation of the Golden Whistle Award. This award was given to the official who made the most boneheaded call or mistake during the previous season. Specifically, he told me, unequivocally, to stop picking on his friend during the award presentation. I simply replied to tell his friend to stop screwing up and he would no longer be a part of the presentation.

I ended the phone call with a laugh. I reached into the cooler for a beer and told Skip to get me home. He asked me what the phone call was about. I gave him the details and he laughed out loud. I quickly reminded him that if he didn't quit screwing up, he would be a part of future programs too. Skip quietly got back to the task at hand, getting me home safely.

THE CRANE KICK

During the early 2000s, Arkansas had a punter who went through an unusual pre-snap routine. When the kicking team got to the line of scrimmage, the punter would take his position behind the center. He then stretched one leg out behind him and took both arms and extended them into the air out in front of him and then overhead. It was very strange and drew a lot of attention.

Paul Petrisko and I had a game in Fayetteville one Saturday in October. Arkansas must not have been very good because this guy made several punts in the first half of the game. It was an early kickoff, so it definitely wasn't a high-profile game.

At halftime, Paul and I joked about how the guy looked like Daniel in the movie *The Karate Kid* when he performed the "crane kick." We had watched this movie several times. "Wax on, wax off." "Paint the fence." "Sand the floor." I'm sure you know the lines too. Prior to the radio systems to communicate during today's games, we used hand signals to indicate various alignments by the offense. An arm stretched out to the side meant the widest player was off the line of scrimmage. A hand held to the side of your face indicated that there was an unbalanced formation with four players lined up on your side of the center. In this situation, the opposite-side official should have a hand on his chest indicating "two for tit."

When games get one-sided and the outcome is obvious, officials have their own routines for staying focused on the tasks at hand. By the fourth quarter, this game was over. Arkansas was getting their ass kicked. Thankfully, the visiting team pulled the starters and substituted the second- and third-string players. Even still, Arkansas had to punt.

Out comes the kicking team. The punter was going through his routine when Paul looks across the field at me to make sure our hand signals were in sync, he began shaking his head back and forth, telling me to stop what I was doing. I had struck the perfect "crane kick" pose, mimicking the Arkansas kicker. I didn't do it quickly and put it down, I held it for at least five seconds. But by the grace of God, Jefferson Pilot didn't catch it and share it to those watching the game from home.

When I was in full pose, the guy that operated the down indicator behind me cracked up laughing. "I've seen that! Spectacular!" Anyway, it was my way of staying focused. Unfortunately, I think I knocked Paul off his game.

BIG RAP SINGERS

I worked my first SEC championship game in December of 2002. This was the tenth anniversary of the game that was first played in Birmingham, Alabama. After two were played there, the annual showdown was moved to Atlanta, where it remains today.

For the officials selected to work the game, it is a great experience. The top-performing crew during the previous season is chosen to officiate the game. Occasionally, changes must be made due to conflicts of interest. If an official is an alumnus of a particular school, they are not allowed to work their games. Not only is this true for the championship game but it pertains to regular-season games as well. But normally, the whole crew handles the game.

When the game is assigned, almost everything is handled by the SEC office. The only task to be taken care of by the individual calling the game is their means of travel. For me, living just north of Atlanta meant a short drive into downtown.

The conference provides a room for three nights at the Hyatt-Regency on Peachtree Street. It's in a block of rooms close to the hospitality suite that is open for most of the weekend. You are provided with tickets to all the events, including four tickets to the game itself.

My son and daughter, on a couple of occasions, have stayed in my room while I drove back and forth from home or rode the train into downtown. With the hospitality suite open, they could get all the food and drinks they needed. It was a special weekend for them.

What Bobby and Gail Gaston started years ago, back in 1994, continues today on a much larger scale. As supervisor of officials, Bobby and his wife, Gail, hosted a small gathering of the officials that were selected to officiate the game at the downtown Capital City Club. From a small group of twenty-five or so, the Friday evening dinner is now attended by a crowd close to two hundred. All the Southeastern Conference football officials are encouraged to attend the banquet. The format of the banquet has stayed consistent over the years.

There is a cocktail reception prior to the dinner. The president of the Southeastern Conference Officials Association opens the dinner with a few remarks and recognitions. The supervisor of officials then summarizes the year and introduces the crew selected to work the game, along with their family and special guests.

The highlight of the evening is the presentation of the Gaston-Dudley Spirit of Officiating Award given to an official that exemplifies the criteria of the award. Following the dinner is a reception in the hospitality suite that can run on into the early morning hours. It's really a very special evening.

During the weekend of this first game for me, "Diamond Jim" Buchanan, the back judge on our crew, gathered everyone together. He had a friend who loved college football. This friend was also a songwriter/musician. Jim handed each of us a CD in its own plastic case. On the CD was a song written and performed by his friend.

Essentially, it was a rap song about our crew and the journey experienced along the way of being assigned the championship game. Each member was mentioned in the song, by either their given name or their nickname. I was referred to as "Gus-O-Matic."

At the time, I thought it was a nice gesture. But as time passed, I've come to appreciate the fact that someone with the same passion for the sport that I have was able to express themselves in a way that only they could.

The song didn't make it on the *Billboard* Hot 100, but it was certainly deserving of that type of recognition. I've still got the original CD.

I'M GONNA PUT THAT IN MY BAG OF TRICKS

In November of 2007, I worked the Alabama-LSU game in Tuscaloosa. It was hyped as a big game. This was the first time Nick Saban would coach against his former team since returning to the SEC as head coach of the Crimson Tide.

My son, August, and a friend of his came over from Starkville, Mississippi, for the game. Both were students at Mississippi State. They met us at the hotel and rode to and from the stadium in the officials' caravan.

The game was broadcast on CBS. It took four hours and twenty minutes to complete the game. Until a late score by LSU, it looked like the game was going to go into overtime. Due to the previously mentioned hype, the kickoff time was moved to four o'clock central time. Three thirty is traditionally the start time for games of this significance.

Games like this are usually easier to officiate due to the players' focus on the field. There's not much pushing and shoving that goes on. Neither team can afford costly penalties. The players know it, and it is reinforced from the coaches.

During this game, LSU had a low-level graduate assistant coach that decided he wanted to act in a role above his pay grade. He made sarcastic comments just far enough away from me so he wouldn't draw too much attention. Or so he thought. He also started to drift into the white area in front of the coach's area on the sidelines. In other words, he was becoming a real pain in the ass.

Late in the third quarter, CBS took a commercial break,

and this provided the opportunity I needed to hopefully make a lasting impression on this young assistant. Brad Freeman was the alternate official for this game. It's always a good idea to have a "witness" when you need to have a conversation with a coach. Brad was standing right next to the guy I needed to have a word with. I casually walked over to him without causing any concern from either one of them.

I calmly asked this guy what his name was. At first, he hesitated. Then, with a smart-ass tone, he asked me why I needed to know. My reply was very simple and direct. "Because the first thing Coach Miles is going to ask me is who the unsportsmanlike conduct foul was on. I need to be able to tell him who it is."

The rest of the game was crickets from this guy's mouth. Back at the hotel, Brad thought that was the greatest technique to get a guy off your ass. He said he was going to put that in his "bag of tricks"! Brad is now an NFL official.

IT'S STARTING
TO GET DARK

During the spring of 1988, I went to Starkville, Mississippi, with my dad. He had knee surgery a few weeks earlier. There was a scrimmage at Mississippi State, and I was going to take his place on the field. I had only worked two years of high school football at that time. I had no concept of college football from an officiating standpoint.

I dressed in the locker room with the other men that were assigned to work the practice. I felt totally out of place. But I knew what was expected of me and I would do my best to live up to those expectations. Officiating college football had never entered my mind at this point. I was officiating just to have something to do in what little spare time I had.

We walked out onto the field in State's stadium, and I was really impressed with how big it looked from ground level. It didn't have an upper deck back then. The grass was in perfect condition. I had never set foot on anything like it before, much less on a football field. There was only one problem, and it was kind of important: There was not a line anywhere.

Jimmy Harper, the referee, tells me, "Hell, we don't need any lines."

I replied, "Well, how are we going to know if they make a first down?"

"The coaches will let us know." I'm beginning to wonder if the coaches even need us.

Rocky Felker was the head coach at State. He had taken over the program from Emory "Make Emory a memory" Bellard. Though older than me, he seemed young to be a head coach. He introduced himself to me after saying "hello" to the other officials. He then turned his attention back to his team.

The script for the scrimmage gets started with the kicking game. The teams run about five kickoffs and ten or so punts. There is no tackling, just touching of the kick receiver once he catches the ball.

The coaches have the players go through about forty-five minutes of walk-throughs. They are lining up on offense and defense. Then specific plays are explained, and they designate which players are going to be blocked, where they want to runner to go, etc. Pretty boring stuff for an official.

Finally, the real scrimmage starts. It's real football. The players are much bigger and faster than what I had experienced at the high school level. We, as officials, are doing the best we can without the lines.

At one point during the practice, I notice that the back judge, Billy Teas, is not on the field. I don't think much about it at the time. Maybe he had to go to the bathroom or something. Then I spot him. He's over by the fence surrounding the field. He's kind of leaning on the fence with his left arm while holding a cigarette in his right hand. He's smoking. It was one of the thin, brown-type cigarettes. This was not what they were teaching me at the high school level.

At the three-and-a-half-hour mark of the practice, Coach Felker calls the players up. *The scrimmage must be over*, I thought to myself. He spoke with his team for a few minutes. Then he tells them that he wants the offense on the five-yard line and the defense to line up. They are going to run goal-line plays.

Jimmy Harper loudly exclaims, "God dammit!" Me being shocked is an understatement. But, apparently, Jimmy had somewhere to go and someone to see. The scrimmage at State was ruining his plans.

Finally, after four hours, we're done. I had worked the longest practice I had ever heard of, even when I played.

There were no lines on the field. I experienced behavior by officials that I had been previously told was completely unacceptable. And besides that, it was starting to get dark.

My dad and I drove back to Atlanta. I crawled into bed around two o'clock in the morning. I fell asleep with the image of Billy Teas taking a break from the scrimmage, leaning on the fence in Starkville, smoking a cigarette.

THAT'S OKAY, THEY'LL BE ON *SportsCenter*

There's only one team that I might show interest in as far as wins and losses go. That would be the Majors from Millsaps College, my alma mater. I just don't watch much football on TV. Officials watch a game differently than the average fan. Yes, we watch players do their thing. We also watch how the balls are switched out between series. We look at the officials' pre-snap position and how they rotate during the play. We criticize how they execute a first-down measurement. You get the idea. Plus, listening to the announcers is painful. Most have no clue about the rules and some of their comments make no sense. Because of this, their lack of knowledge borders on the absurd.

On October 27, 2007, I was in Knoxville, Tennessee, for the Volunteers' game against South Carolina. Also playing this weekend was Millsaps College. Their opponent was the Tigers from Trinity College out of San Antonio, Texas. The game was played on Harper Davis Field in Jackson, Mississippi.

Both teams were ranked in the top twenty-five of Division III football. The winner would likely go on to represent their conference in the Division III playoffs. I had interest in the outcome of the game and had no way of getting updates during the afternoon as we prepared for our game in Knoxville.

Once we arrived at Neyland Stadium to begin our pregame duties, Chris Conley and I were walking around on the Tennessee sideline. ESPN was covering our game that evening. Holly Rowe was assigned as the on-field reporter. Chris and I stopped to speak with Holly. As we were getting ready to walk over to the other side of the field, I asked Holly if she could find out how the Millsaps game ended. She certainly had more important things to do and I don't think she really took me seriously. Chris started giving me a hard time about how insignificant that game was, and no one really cared.

Realizing that I probably wasn't going to get any updates, I calmly replied, "That's okay, it'll be on *SportsCenter* later tonight." We went about our business and worked a pretty good ball game. Tennessee won the game over the Gamecocks, 27–24.

After the game, we returned to our hotel. We showered and wrapped up our pregame meeting quickly. Some of the crew met up in someone's room to watch TV and catch up on the results of the other games around the league. It was late and all the East Coast games had finished for the evening. There was a West Coast game being played and, occasionally, we would switch channels and watch a little of it.

Finally, ESPN's *SportsCenter* came on. They would go through all the games, one by one, and then I could go to bed. I didn't have a smartphone back in those days, so I had no way of checking on the outcome of the Millsaps-Trinity game. Hopefully, I would get some information, even though it was not major college action.

Chris and I were sitting on the end of the bed, right in front of the TV. ESPN was coming out of a commercial break to begin their next segment. The music ramped up, they showed a shot of the studio and panned in on the two commentators behind a fancy desk. Everyone in our room turned their attention to the TV.

The first game they covered was the Millsaps game. Chris Conley almost fell off the bed. I simply said, "See? I told you they'd be on *SportsCenter*," while trying to not sound completely shocked.

The studio commentators began saying, "You are not going to believe it when you see the following play out of Jackson, Mississippi, earlier this afternoon." They laid the background for the video clip they were going to show. Millsaps had the lead, 24–22. The Majors had an opportunity to win the game if they could convert just one first down in the final two minutes of the game. Instead, failing to do so, they left two seconds on the game clock.

Trinity had an opportunity for one final play from their own forty-yard line. The Tigers lined up and snapped the ball. One forward pass, one fumble, and fifteen laterals later, Trinity was in the endzone for the game-winning touchdown. The play lasted sixty-two seconds. At one point during the play, someone lit the fireworks in the endzone thinking Millsaps had won the game.

Everyone in our room had just witnessed the "Miracle in Mississippi" with the wrong team winning the game. Millsaps wouldn't make the playoffs that year.

My crewmates started giving me a really hard time. I simply stood up, told them, "Go pound sand, and good night!" I went to my room, dejected.

THE FOOD COMA

Some rituals are worth repeating—seriously. One such ritual rolled around every year during the SEC summer pre-season clinic. The format of the clinic went something like this: Everyone arrives in Birmingham around lunch on a Thursday during the last weekend of July. Thursday evening, the rules test is taken. Early on Friday morning, the physical assessment was completed.

The physical assessment is made up of a quick weigh-in and blood-pressure check by a team of doctors and athletic trainers. Groups of twelve officials, one after another, run a timed mile and a half. The older officials get to go first, and the first group to run starts around 6:15.

For all intents and purposes, the clinic is over at the conclusion of the run. The only thing left is listening to endless talking and watching videos in a dark room.

After everyone has completed the run, the next agenda item doesn't start until one p.m. There's plenty of time to get back to the hotel in order to clean up and go to lunch.

Over the span of some twenty years, a group of twenty or thirty guys would make the trek to Dreamland Bar-B-Que. Dreamland is an iconic restaurant that specializes in hickory-smoked ribs, white loaf bread, and BBQ sauce. This location in Birmingham would recognize us as we arrived. They provide an upstairs room that will easily accommodate everyone. Our arrival time was usually a little before eleven a.m.

Over the course of the next hour and a half, we would devour slabs of ribs and endless pieces of bread. Of course, it had to be washed down. Some teetotalers would have sweet tea or cokes. Most would have a nice, ice-cold longneck beer. Some would have several.

After asking for one check, everyone would pitch in. The one waitress would earn a several-hundred-dollar tip. Everyone was in a good mood.

The group then made the return trek back to the hotel conference room for the rest of Friday's agenda. Any updates, clarifications, and announcements would be made first. Then the talking and video sessions would commence. If you sat toward the back of the room, you could see the bobblehead action from the folks that hit Dreamland when the lights were turned down. The clinic was pretty much over.

Update: The mile-and-a-half run has been done away with. Time will tell before the SEC football officials start looking out of shape.

WELL, THAT DIDN'T GO AS PLANNED

In 1992, the Southeastern Conference Football Officials Association decided it was time to unionize and be deemed employees of the conference. Over the three years since Roy Kramer had become the commissioner, he had let the officials know that, in no uncertain terms, they were just a necessary evil, and he would never support them if a coach ever made a complaint against one of us. It was time for action. We'll show them.

A small group of officials within the organization began putting a plan in place. This group was made up of guys that were the most pissed off at the commissioner. The referees of the crews were going to be the conduit for spreading the information. Those officials, like myself, who were not on specific crews, were contacted by a veteran and were kept informed by them. My contact was Butch Lambert Jr.

On paper, things looked to make sense. However, emotions pushed common sense aside. Were the officials underpaid? Yes. Had fees kept up with the increase in the cost of living? No. Did the officials feel appreciated by the league office? No.

As happens in society, a small group of self-interested individuals can whip a crowd into a frenzy and persuade them to do things they wouldn't normally do. Personally, I saw solidarity in the officiating organization, and I wanted to support it. To my knowledge, we only had one outspoken member who did not go along with the group: an official from Gordo, Alabama.

Remembering back, the group never heard directly from the people who would legally represent us in this endeavor. The spread of information was slow and not completely accurate. Over the course of a week and many telephone calls, the consensus was reached to hire Richie Phillips to represent the organization.

Richie Phillips had represented many union organizations, two of which were the Major League Baseball umpires and National Basketball Association referees. Being from Philadelphia, Pennsylvania, and having a reputation of being a hard-nose lawyer, how could we go wrong?

Over the course of many months, information was gathered at the request of Phillips's law firm. When it was time, a motion was filed that requested a hearing with the National Labor Relations Board. Due to the location of the conference office, the hearing would be held in Birmingham, Alabama.

While all of this was going on in the background, the season was in full swing, and we were officiating games. The league office did have concerns that we may strike at any time. We didn't have the desire to do that. We just wanted to be treated fairly. Rumor had it that the commissioner had shadow crews of officials ready to go in the event of a strike. That was never confirmed.

As the season went on, you could feel the tension building between our supervisor, Bobby Gaston, and the officials' association. Information about what was going on spread. Coaches and sports writers began to find out what was happening. It was beginning to take on a life of its own.

The time came for the parties involved to begin to bring this to a resolution. There were never any good-faith negotiations. Cooler heads would have said, "Hey, can we just sit down and see if we can work some of these concerns out?" It was really a matter of "We'll show them!" from both sides.

When the day finally arrived for the first hearings with the NLRB, Richie Phillips apparently thought it was going to be a slam dunk. His confidence was so high that he didn't person-ally attend the hearing. He sent in his lieutenants. The Southeastern Conference lawyered up big time. We were on their turf, and they were not going to play patsy.

In short order, after calling just a few witnesses, we were handed our rear ends in a sling. We were blown out of the water. The entire hearing lasted just over two hours.

For some reason unknown to me, we were not all let go and replaced. A couple of people quit but most of us were still around.

Our relationship with the conference changed. Independ-ent-contractor agreements became the norm and if you didn't sign their contract, you didn't work. When we were provided whistles with the SEC logo on it, we were explicitly told that these were only gifts, and we were not "required" to use them. One of the things that bothered me the most was that we were no longer listed in the conference media guide as officials. I always thought that was pretty cool.

Some officials pushed back. There was a game at Auburn officiated by Mac Gentry's crew. While inspecting the field, Mac noticed a network camera mounted on a large tripod just off the endline in the back of the endzone. Commissioner Kramer was also on the field and Mac brought this problem to his attention. The commissioner didn't see it as a problem and informed Mac to play the game.

Gentry told the commissioner that he had two choices: put in writing that he was taking responsibility for the placement of camera or have it moved. If he didn't do one of these, the game would not be played. The commissioner was not going to take liability for anything, so the camera was moved.

It took many years for the effects of our actions to finally calm down. The one person that I felt the sorriest for was Bobby Gaston, the supervisor of officials. He had been an of-ficial. He was our guy and we let him down. He always did everything possible to support us. Yes, he worked for the conference, but he had our best interests at heart and did all he could to help us. We put him in a position of trying to balance the impossible. We had made a big mistake. There was only Plan A. It didn't work out.

205

They say you can call a foul on every play. That's true, but most non-safety fouls don't cause a competitive disadvantage for the opponent. For example, let's say you have a toss sweep to the left side of the offense. On the back side, away from the play, the offensive tackle may reach and grab a defender. With both players clearly out of the play, you won't see that holding foul called. At least, you shouldn't. Now, if the tackle were to grab him by his facemask, that would be called. So, there are subtle differences.

On October 7, 2006, I was in Athens for the Tennessee versus Georgia game. The first half was all Georgia and they led 24–14 at the break. During the second half, Tennessee outscored the Bulldogs, 37–9, for a final score of 51–33. Russ Pulley, our umpire, hadn't called a foul during the entire game. With the game out of Georgia's hands, both teams started substituting their second- and third-string players in the middle of the fourth quarter.

As officials, we're just trying to get the game over with. The coaches were still coaching but they were running simple plays and trying to avoid any injuries to players.

During one such running play up the middle by Georgia, the losing team, Pulley throws his flag for holding. When he reports the foul to the referee, Steve Shaw looks at him with exasperation and says something like, "Really?"

Pulley says, "It was so bad, I had to call it."

I'm standing there needing to get penalty information to move the chains and I look up at the scoreboard. There's two minutes and five seconds remaining in the game.

From that moment on through the present, Pulley's nickname became "205."

BLESS YOUR HEART

I believe it was at the beginning of 2015 when the Southeastern Conference invited the first female to attend the annual football officials' summer clinic in Birmingham. It might have been 2016 but the date really doesn't matter.

As is the case with all these meetings, there are numerous breaks throughout the day. To keep people from wandering off too far, there are beverages and snacks along the sides and rear of the meeting rooms. There is usually an ample supply of cups and ice.

When you settle in for the first meeting, you find yourself sitting with the same people over the course of the weekend. Such was the case during this particular clinic. I spent most of the time sitting close to a friend from Greenville, South Carolina. This guy started officiating in the SEC the year after I began. We were certainly considered veterans at this point in our careers.

During the first break of day one, we went to get something to drink. There was a wide variety of soft drinks, snacks, and ice, but no cups. As we were standing there, this lady walks up and my friend politely asks if she can go get some more Styrofoam cups. She walks off obviously hearing the question but never returned with more cups. We each just grabbed a can and returned to our seats.

Usually, at the start of the meetings, the coordinator of officials will introduce the individuals who are attending for the first time. Steve Shaw was the coordinator during this period of time. He started on the other side of the room from where we were sitting. One by one, Steve would call out someone's name and have them stand up. Eventually, he worked his way over to our side of the room.

He mentioned something about having a special guest with us from a somewhat historical perspective. He then asked this female official to please stand up. On the row in front of us, three chairs down was the lady that my friend had asked to bring us some more cups. He slowly lowered his head. Fortunately, the applause from the group in the room drowned out my laughter.

He had made an honest mistake. Our "special guest" was wearing a black pantsuit that very closely resembled the outfits that the staff of the Marriott hotel wore. He had missed one critical item: she didn't have a Marriott name badge on. He apologized to her at his first opportunity.

Still, it took me the rest of the afternoon to remove this guy's foot from his mouth. So much for good first impressions.

BOBBY SAID I COULD WEAR THEM

Without a doubt, Paul "Paulette" Petrisko was my closest friend throughout my officiating career. He still is, to this day. He's the kind of guy that can take and deliver the same amount of friendly abuse as me. We rag on each other constantly when we're together.

In the mid-2000s, Paulette had a game where Tennessee was playing at Arkansas. It was a very sunny, fall afternoon. With an early kickoff, the white areas on the field are really bright. To the point where you must squint when you're out there until your eyes get adjusted. Then, at halftime when you go back in the locker room, things seem darker than normal. After a little time passes, you can begin to see normal again. This repeats itself when you return to the field for the second half.

Traditionally, SEC officials did things "old school." We didn't wear gloves or ear protection during cold weather. You didn't wear any extra protection during rainy games. And you damn sure didn't wear sunglasses, period. The perception was that it would impair your vision.

Well, Paulette persuaded Bobby Gaston, our supervisor of officials, to wear sunglasses during the previously mentioned game. He used the excuse that the sunlight was hurting his sensitive eyes.

The next day, the front page of the sports section showed a close-up of Paulette running down the sideline with his sunglasses on. Immediately in front of him was the Arkansas runner and Tennessee defender. The runner had the defender's facemask wrapped up in his hand. And I mean *bad* wrapped up. The Tennessee player was almost looking out of the ear hole in the helmet.

It's rarely called but you can certainly have a facemask penalty against the runner. It's one thing to stiff arm a player but they cannot grasp any opening of the helmet or the facemask itself.

So, there is Paulette, sunglasses on, player committing an unbelievably obvious facemask foul, and what does he do? Nothing, no foul.

This earned Paulette the Golden Whistle Award. And sunglasses have not been worn since.

HOW TO
DELIVER A JOKE

Some people just have that knack for being able to tell a joke. Ray Moon was one of those people. Ray took me under his wing when I got into the Southeastern Conference. He showed me the important "ropes." When my kids' mother and I were going through our divorce in 1996, he called and checked on me. He asked me what I was going to do for Christmas. Not having any real plans, he told me I was going to go to Montgomery, Alabama, and officiate the Blue-Grey All Star Game on Christmas Day. There's not much traffic on I-285 and I-85 early on Christmas morning.

During the summer clinic of 1998, Ray had a joke that I heard him tell several times. It was his "Joke of the Weekend"! Each time he repeated it, the funnier it got. It was somewhat colorful and should probably have only been told to only certain audiences.

Traditionally, on the Friday evening during the clinic weekends, a group of four to eight couples would go out to dinner at a very nice restaurant. Gramaci's was the name of one such place. This particular evening our party consisted of twelve people. Ray's wife, Luanne, was with us. Her nickname was "The Claw." During dinner, we noticed Charlie Pell and his wife having dinner across the room. Charlie had been the head coach at Florida many years before. Jimmy Harper and Bob "Turkey" Lee got up and went to talk with Coach Pell. When Mrs. Pell recognized our table of other officials, she came over to speak with us. She reminisced about her time in Gainesville and how she missed being around the league.

Ray tells Mrs. Pell that he was also going to miss being around SEC football because he was going to retire after that upcoming season. She replies, "Ray, you don't look that old." Unknown to her, she had just placed Ray up on his personal stage, spotlight and all. Everyone at the table was thinking the same thing. There's no way in *hell* that Ray was going to tell her his "joke of the weekend"! We were frozen, subconsciously pleading, *Please don't do it!*

"You know why I don't look so old?" Ray asked.

"No," says Mrs. Pell.

"Because my pecker is so big, it pulls all the wrinkles out of my face."

The Claw screams "Ray!" at the top her lungs. Mrs. Pell acts like that is the funniest thing she's heard in a long time. I think she needed it.

HOW'S THE BOAT?

In 2005, LSU's home game against Appalachian State was postponed due to Hurricane Katrina. South Louisiana and South Mississippi had been devastated by this destructive storm. LSU and the city of Baton Rouge was essentially converted into a triage for the people that had fled New Orleans and other places in south Louisiana.

This was Les Miles first season at LSU. It would prove to be more than a challenge. His second game against Arizona State was to be a home game also. Due to conditions in Baton Rouge, from both a facilities and psychological standpoint, the game was moved to Tempe, Arizona.

LSU had a bye week already scheduled for the weekend of September 17. They would have two weeks to prepare for their next home game against Tennessee on Saturday, the twenty-fourth.

The week leading up to the game against the Vols showed another hurricane spinning around in the Gulf of Mexico. The plans for the game were still on. The storm looked like it was going to track more to the west and miss New Orleans and Baton Rouge.

Because of this storm, the assigned crew was told to get into Baton Rouge on Thursday due to the slight chance that the game might be played earlier. Well, Hurricane Rita had other plans. She made a turn north and hit south Louisiana where it meets Texas. Conditions in Baton Rouge got too bad to play on Saturday. The game would be played, but not until Monday evening, September 26.

The guys on this crew were holed up in the hotel having to endure periodic power outages and other terrible conditions.

ESPN was planning on broadcasting the LSU-Tennessee game but when the game was moved to Monday night, ESPN sent their crew to Starkville, Mississippi, to cover the Georgia at Mississippi State game, where I would officiate that day.

Earlier during the day of our game, I ran into some of the ESPN people. They were staying at the same hotel as me. We sat in the lobby and talked about where they had come from and the changes that were made. I mentioned that we had a crew stuck in a hotel in Baton Rouge with nothing to do.

The producer for ESPN began telling me that, because of the hotel situations in Baton Rouge, they had chartered one of the cruise-line paddle-wheel boats on the Mississippi River. It was essentially empty, as this crew wouldn't return until Sunday to begin preparing for the Monday broadcast at LSU. He said to me, "Tell your guys to call me and they can stay out on the boat with us. We've got more than enough rooms for everyone." He gave me all his contact information along with a contact of a person that had stayed behind on the boat.

When I got back to my room, I called the referee of the crew in Baton Rouge to relay the information. I gave them names and telephone numbers of the people they should call. ESPN had a van and offered to take them from the hotel to the boat.

After our game on Saturday evening, I drove home, leaving Starkville early on Sunday morning. When I got home and unpacked all my gear, I decided to give the crew in Baton Rouge a call and see how the boat was. The referee answered the phone, and my first question was, "How are things going?"

He begins describing how the hotel is, that the power goes off and on, there's no cable TV. Things are not good. "Why aren't y'all on the boat?" I asked.

There was a pause on the other end. He didn't answer me right away. After a little more conversation, I figured out that they thought I was playing a practical joke on them when I gave them the ESPN information the morning before. Who, me? I would never play a joke on anyone! Ha! This time, I was serious.

This crew never called anybody. To justify not going to the boat, they claimed that they didn't want to hurt the feelings of the people running the hotel there in Baton Rouge.

Anyway, it was too late, the game was the next day. But at first light on Tuesday morning following the game, the officials in Baton Rouge left the hotel as fast as possible. Damn the feelings of the hotel staff.

I HEARD IT
TOUCH HIM

Crowd noise can be deafening at times. This is true at any SEC venue, even Vanderbilt. When there's a lot on the line, the noise starts well before kickoff.

On November 11, 1995, Auburn traveled to Athens to play Georgia. Both teams were in need of a win to become bowl eligible. There was much at stake, including the job security of the head coaches.

Athens, Georgia, was alive. The weather was cold and windy for the evening kickoff. ESPN put the game in their prime-time slot. Patrick Nix was the quarterback for Auburn. Hines Ward and Brian Smith were substituting at quarterback for Georgia. These two had taken over for Mike Bobo after he was hurt at Ole Miss earlier in the season. Brad Nessler and the always outspoken Gary Danielson were the commentators for the broadcast.

Auburn jumped into the lead, late in the first quarter. With a little over ten minutes remaining in the second quarter, Auburn was up, 13–0. It felt like Auburn was the better team, but Georgia played well. Each time the Bulldogs had some success, Auburn would answer. Georgia was down, 31–34, with about six minutes left to play. Inside the Auburn fifteen-yard line, Georgia went for it on fourth and seven, instead of kicking a field goal to tie. Georgia didn't convert, Auburn took over, went down the field, and kicked a field goal for the final score of the game. Auburn ended up winning the game, 37–31.

Bobby "Poof" Caldwell was the line judge in the game. He

worked on the line of scrimmage opposite of me. Bobby was a Georgia Tech graduate. I always wondered why he didn't scratch Georgia and not work their games. The nickname "Poof" came around because there were times where a small group of people would be gathered and talking. All of sudden, Bobby would be gone. He wouldn't say anything to anyone. He would just do the "walk off"! It was like he vanished into thin air–"Poof!"

Bobby was a good official but sometimes things would happen that would make you scratch your head. That, along with his great sense of humor, made him a fun guy to be around.

In the third quarter of this game, Poof had one of his greatest moments. Auburn was set to punt on fourth down. The kick is short, hits an Auburn player on his leg, and the ball rolls downfield a little farther, where Georgia recovers. Instead of the ball being awarded to Georgia at the point of recovery, the ball is returned to the spot where it hit the Auburn player. This spot is called the spot of first touching.

Poof made the first-touching call from about twenty-five yards away from where it occurred. When he reported the situation to Bill Goss, our referee, Bill quizzed him about what had happened. Bill then asked him how it was he saw the action while the downfield officials didn't. Poof replied, "I heard the ball hit the player!"

During the preseason summer clinic of 1995, I had been awarded the Golden Whistle Award. This award is not for something from a great-officiating performance. It's more for a bonehead-type situation that occurred during or around a game. The protocol of the award required the previous year's winner to make the presentation to the succeeding year's recipient.

After Bill learned about the touching that Poof "heard," he called a time out, motioning me to come over to where they were standing. In Bill's calm demeanor, he told Poof to tell me what he had reported about the touching. Without missing a beat, Poof repeated it. My reaction was, "What, no way!"

Goss asked me if I understood what I had been told. "Yes, I heard what he told me."

Bill then told me, "Good, I want to nominate Bobby for next year's Golden Whistle Award." The next year, Poof did win the Golden Whistle Award, to much fanfare.

As a side note, this game was also the last home game to be played between the original famed hedges. The field was going to be reconfigured to accommodate for soccer during the 1996 Summer Olympics. Fans began taking pieces of the hedges during the game for keepsakes.

Also, Ray Goff was fired at the conclusion of the season, which was his seventh as the head coach of Georgia.

I ONLY HAVE ONE STIPULATION

Sharing rooms with other officials helps with the amount of money you spend while traveling for games. Within crews, it's usually the same couple of guys that share rooms week after week, season after season. I shared more rooms with Mike Shirey over the years than he's probably shared with his wife.

Guys with similar habits usually end up splitting rooms. The only stipulation I have is that the other person *cannot* snore, period.

Back in the mid '90s, I was scheduled to work with another crew in a game at Kentucky. The official I split the room with on Friday night was able to drive home after the game. So another official, Cleve Hale, checked out of his room and moved into mine. Cleve was from the Atlanta area. He assured me he didn't snore before we made the transition.

Because our game was an early kickoff that Saturday, we had plenty of time to make plans for dinner that evening. There was a very good steak restaurant catty-cornered from the hotel in downtown Lexington. deSha's had the best prime rib I had ever eaten. When Cleve asked me what I was going to do for dinner, I told him, "deSha's." He decided to go with me. It's literally a hundred-foot walk from the door of the hotel.

We got a table and ordered a couple of beers. They had these honey-flavored muffins that they put on the table while you're waiting on the main course. I already knew what I wanted, so there was no need for me to read over the menu.

Cleve was a little undecided, at first, but settled on a ribeye. You got a fresh salad and a side to go with it.

The meal came out perfectly. We talked about the game as we ate our meal. When we were through, we walked back to the hotel for the evening. It was getting late, so we turned in shortly after we got up to the room. This was around 10:30.

Sometime shortly after midnight, a freight train rolled through the room. Cleve began to snore at a volume rarely achieved by any human being. I would call out his name and he would stop snoring for a few minutes. About the time I would drift off to sleep, the train would make another pass through the room. I hardly slept at all that night.

The next morning, after Cleve woke up, I asked him why he told me that he didn't snore. He said he didn't. I told him about my evening of no sleep, and he said the only reason he might have snored is because of the red meat he had eaten for dinner. I told him that if red meat causes that to happen, he should never, *ever* eat it again. No one should be subjected to that again, period.

IT HAPPENED DURING FOOTBALL SEASON

In 2009, the SEC hosted its third championship-game-weekend hospitality suite under the supervision of its then-coordinator of officials. As had been the case for the previous two years, the hospitality suite events were "alcohol free!" When you are the man, you can call the shots. But officiating football and drinking beer are almost synonymous.

To be fair, the coordinator did call me and tell me that he had no problem with the officials' association having some-what of a suite of our own, at a different hotel. We did. Skip Ramsey and I bootlegged twenty-five cases of beer, wrapped in Christmas paper, through the lobby of the Marriott Marquis hotel in downtown Atlanta.

Over the weekend, I thought it would be fun to set up interviews with fellow officials. The purpose was to have them narrate their most entertaining story about what went on in a particular game of theirs. It went well, except for the background noise of those in the hospitality suite. People were having a fun time at our "alcohol included" event.

Then it was Mike New's turn. He took his place in front of the camera and began spinning a tale that was absolutely unbelievable. It involved a wedding that he and his wife had attended. His story told of a speech by the future father-in-law. He absolutely trashed the bride. At some point, he even used the term of endearment, "Slut!" Mike is a remarkable teller of tales. A crowd had gathered behind the camera and hung on every word that came out of his mouth. After about five minutes, he concluded his story by saying, "The end."

When he finished, I asked him, "What in the *hell* does that have to do with football?" As he was getting up from the chair in front of camera, he replied, "Oh, it happened during football season."

JIMMY HARPER

During the 1991 season, I was assigned to work the clock during an LSU game in Baton Rouge. It was my first trip to Tiger Stadium.

I was in awe of the atmosphere around the game. I was working with a veteran crew led by the referee, Jimmy Harper. When Jimmy was on the field, you knew who was in charge.

The game itself is somewhat of blur to me. One, I was a young guy around really good officials. Two, operating the game clock is damn sure not as easy as it looks. It requires intense concentration and it's easy to screw up. (I didn't mess it up that night.) Three, watching the Golden Girls do their thing is mesmerizing. And the last thing that really impressed me was the ride to and from the stadium.

The deputies of East Baton Rouge parish provide the most exciting escort of any group throughout the conference. When everyone is loaded in one of their prisoner-transport vans, they haul ass out of the parking lot led by several motorcycle units. These guys are fearless. The motorcade turns right on Acadia Boulevard toward I-10, then the magic begins. They execute a flawless rolling roadblock.

The van drivers never stop during the drive to the stadium, even at red lights. Intersections are blocked as the escort blows through them. Finally, the vehicles stop between the Maravich Center and Tiger Stadium where the officials unload and go into their locker room.

During our trip to the stadium for my first trip to Tiger Stadium, I was sitting on the second row of seats behind the driver. Jimmy Harper was riding shotgun. He had earned that position.

When we made our switch on Nicholson Drive back over to the southbound lanes, a blue Toyota Celica hatchback had to jump the curb to get out of our way. Either that or get run over. When the car's rear wheels hit the curb, out flew a keg of beer, hitting the ground.

Without missing a beat, Jimmy says in his deep southern accent, "They won't be drinking any of that for a while!" He sounded as if he felt sorry for them. I sure did because you know they had a crowd waiting on them to get there.

NO, YOU'RE NOT GOING

In 2004, I became an avid scuba diver. I loved it. It was a great way to relax. My wife was in total agreement, only if I bought the best and most reliable equipment. And I did.

I dove in the Gulf of Mexico, various lakes, quarries, and the crystal-clear waters surrounding Eleuthera. I just thoroughly enjoyed the different experiences and the quietness of being underwater. I always had a reliable dive buddy.

In September of 2005, my first game of the season was in Gainesville, Florida. It was Labor Day weekend. I sent an email out to the crew that I was going diving while I was there and if anyone wanted to join me, please let me know. Russ Pulley, the umpire on the crew, sent a reply saying, "I'm in!"

For this weekend, I packed my scuba equipment along with my officiating gear. I drove to Gainesville on Friday afternoon and had dinner and a short film session with the crew that evening. Our game was scheduled for a seven o'clock kickoff the following evening. That would leave plenty of time for a couple of early-morning dives.

When I ran into Russ at the hotel, I told him that we should leave around six a.m. and be there when they open. Being that it was Labor Day weekend, I figured the place would be packed.

He looked down and the conversation went something like this.

Russ: "I can't go."

Me: "What?"

Russ: "Steve won't let me go."

Me: "He didn't tell me I couldn't go."

Russ: "I asked Steve if he told you not to go either and he said no. I asked him then why just me, and he said, 'You're not Gus.'" I had been in the league for a long time at that point but if Steve Shaw told me he didn't want me to go, trust me, I wouldn't have gone.

The state of Florida has some amazing freshwater springs. Not too far from Gainesville, in the town of Williston, is a diving location called Devil's Den Spring. It's a small hole in the ground out in the middle of nowhere. There's a little dive hut where you register, and if you need air or supplies, you can get it there.

Early that Saturday morning, I headed off to Williston, Florida, alone. When I got there, my car was the only one in the parking area. I went into the dive shop to register. The lady behind the counter said I shouldn't get my hopes up too high about diving that morning. When I asked her why, she said, "It's Labor Day weekend. I don't even know why I open. Nobody ever comes." Shocked as I was, she said, "You can wait for a while and see if anybody shows up. You must have a dive partner to enter the springs."

After an hour, a lone pickup truck pulled into the parking lot. I was hoping that it contained an odd number of people, meaning I would have a dive partner. As luck would have it, out jumped one person. I walked over, introduced myself, and explained the situation for the lack of other divers.

We signed in and got our equipment set up. Over the next couple of hours, we completed two dives. He asked if I wanted to lead. Since I was there to have a relaxing couple of dives, I told him to do his thing and I would just tag along. In between the dives, we sat and chatted. The usual small talk.

Devil's Den is a very nice dive spot. Since it is, in effect, an underground chamber, lights are hanging from the ceiling. It's really pretty cool but did cause me a slight feeling of claustrophobia.

After our second dive, no others had yet shown up. As we were packing our gear away, he asked me, "Are you in town just to dive?"

I said, "No, I'm going to the Florida game tonight."

"Cool, my wife and I are going too. Maybe we'll see you there!"

I replied back, "It's a big crowd but look for a guy with an 'H' on his back." I shook his hand, told him it was nice to meet him, and we bid each other good-bye.

When I was about to pull out of the parking lot, he pulled up beside me, rolled down his window, and asked, "You're a ref?" I put my finger up in front of my lips and said, "Don't tell anyone!"

With that, he gave me an "Oh, wow!" and drove off.

As I pulled back into the hotel, I saw Steve Shaw in the parking lot. I could tell by the look in his eyes that he was relieved to see that I had survived the morning. We ended up working a very good game that evening. I was relaxed from the dive. Steve was relaxed that he was able to work with a full crew.

SHUT UP, NOW

Some people are more skilled than others when it comes to effective communication while using an economy of words. Bill Goss was one of these people. Bill was a Tulane guy and one of the smartest people in the world of officiating. He was a Southeastern Conference referee, who, in the end of his career, got dealt a bad hand.

Bill and I had a game in Monroe, Louisiana, one night. I have no idea who NE Louisiana was playing and, to be honest, it really doesn't matter.

The coach of this unrecallable team was on my ass the entire game. It was relentless. "They're holding," "They're offsides," "They've got too many players in the huddle!" It went on like this before, during, and after every play.

I do remember that the Indians beat the crap out of his team. One particular play had his running back get forced out of bounds on my sideline. The head coach was adamant that there was a late hit. This was the last straw.

In plays like this, the referee runs with the players and helps cover out of bounds plays. Bill followed this action and came into the out-of-bounds area close to where I was.

I felt like I had reinforcements when Bill was with me on the sideline. I said something back to the coach, which probably looked and sounded like, "Now that I've got help, I'll tell you!" Bill immediately told me not to argue with him.

Hearing Bill telling me to be quiet, the coach started squawking at me again. His sounded like, "Yeah, he told you!"

Bill spun around on him and told him, "Shut up, now! I know Gus has had enough because I've had enough and I'm out in the middle of the field." The guy was mad as hell, but he didn't say another word until after the game was over.

Even after all this, I still shook his hand after the game. As I began to walk away, he spouted off one more time: "Y'all suck!" Bill had made his point. I didn't react. Besides, there was absolutely nothing I could do. The game was over, and our jurisdiction had ended.

Later that evening, Bill only made one comment about this situation: "You're better than that." Lesson learned.

THE SLEEPWALKER

Ray Moon was a good bit older than me, but he was the one veteran SEC official that really showed me how to work a game. He wasn't the strongest when it came to rules knowledge, but he could take control during any game. He had earned respect for the coaches and because he organized the coaches' and officials' golf tournaments, he knew most of the assistants.

Ray was one of the funniest guys I have ever been around. He could tell jokes and stories as well as anyone, regardless of the audience.

He had one peculiar trait that, fortunately, most people don't experience. Moon was prone to walk in his sleep. He also ended most phone calls with, "Hey, I've got to go catch this other call."

Ray was divorced but eventually met and married Luanne, a.k.a. the Claw. After they had been dating for a while, he stayed over at her house one evening. During the night, Ray got up from bed and walked into Luanne's closet. Thinking he was in her bathroom, he did his business and went back to bed. I would think most of the time that would be a deal breaker, but I guess she thought he was a keeper and she let it slide.

Toward the end of his football-officiating career, Ray was assigned to work the Liberty Bowl in Memphis, Tennessee. The crew members were provided rooms at one of the larger, sprawling hotels on the outskirts of the city. It was made up of six or eight separate buildings that were connected by open air courtyards.

The bowl committee arranged for the hotel to provide

rooms for not only the officials but for other groups that would be part of the festivities during the game. Making up some of these groups were high school bands that perform on the field before the game, concluding with the playing of the National Anthem. The rooms are usually provided for three nights.

Luanne and Ray went to the Liberty Bowl together—a short get away just prior to New Years. On the first night of the bowl weekend, Ray has one of his sleepwalking episodes. He gets up out of bed, walks out of room, and begins to walk the halls of the hotel. He leaves one building and goes into a courtyard area. Since it's late December, the air outside is very cold. In fact, it's cold enough that Ray awakens and comes out of his sleep. There he stands in his boxer shorts without a clue as to where he is. He begins to realize the gravity of his predicament.

He recognizes which building his room is in and goes into it. The problem is that he doesn't know the room number—Ray had Luanne to remember that type of information. Even if he did remember the room number, he had no way of unlocking the door. There's no place to put a room key in a pair of boxer shorts.

It wasn't very late during his walk, around 11:30, and there are other guests in the hotel that are still up. Ray realizes this when he looks through the glass doors leading outside and sees some of the high school band members loitering around. *Oh, shit!* he thought to himself. To make matters worse, these were female band members.

The doors leading into the rooms were slightly recessed from the hallway. When Ray realized he might be seen, he backed into one of these doors and tried to make himself as small as possible. After the threat of being discovered was over, he began to try to figure out which room was his. Panic was beginning to set in. He wished he was still asleep. A bad dream was better than the situation he was currently in.

Luanne woke up to find that Ray was not in bed. She knew what had happened. She got up, put on some clothes, and went looking for Ray. When she opened the door, there he was. He jumped from the hallway into the room, saying, "I think I'm going back to bed." During breakfast the next morning, he told some of his crewmembers the story from the night before. At some point, someone asked the right question, "Ray, how do you know all of this? You were asleep."

THESE BEERS AREN'T EVEN COLD

The officiating-crew concept started back in 1992. The theory behind the decision was that cohesion would develop between the members of the crew and they would work better as a unit. The first few years of my SEC career were spent as a journeyman. I wasn't assigned to a crew, which to me was great. I got to work with most of the other officials in the league.

My second and third season saw Bobby Gaston, coordinator of officials, put together a quasi-crew of newer officials. We were essentially the "Homecoming Crew." We weren't assigned any real meaningful games, that is, on paper.

As years went by, I was on many different crews. Who knows why? Maybe I wasn't what some people wanted as a crewmate or maybe the crews were jungled around to keep things fresh.

In the early 2000s, I was on one particular crew for three consecutive years. The first two years were a blast. We were pretty good but more importantly, we had a great time. This crew had two back judges. When either of these two guys was not working on the field, they served as the alternate official and ran the game clock. We traveled together as a group of eight.

During the third year of the eight of us being together as a crew, tensions started to build. Things were not as smooth as they had been. We had suffered through a couple of really high-profile miscues during games. We may not have been as prepared as we could have been prior to some games.

Things came to a head on a Friday evening, prior to a game in Fayetteville, Arkansas. Several officials, including myself, were delayed while flying in for the game. Bad weather was all around the Southeast. My itinerary had me leaving Atlanta and connecting through Dallas. My flight arrived in Dallas on time. However, my flight to Fayetteville kept getting pushed back. In fact, it was getting late, and I needed to decide on renting a car to make it to Fayetteville in time to work the game. The Delta Red Coat assured me that we would be leaving eventually. I stayed with my plans and, sure enough, we flew out of Dallas.

The flight didn't land until almost 11:30 p.m. A couple of crewmates drove out to the airport to pick me up. I had given them the time to be there during a phone call as my flight was about to leave Dallas. I also told them to bring me a couple of beers for the ride to the hotel.

When I got to the car, the front passenger seat was empty, so I jumped in to ride shotgun. There were two longneck Budweisers on the floorboard of the car. "Shit, these aren't even cold," I exclaimed. The reply I got was weird. Normally, I would have gotten a sarcastic response back. But not this time. Something was up. Or maybe it was just late. I finished both beers by the time we got to the hotel.

The night's sleep was short due to our six a.m. pregame meeting. I got up, showered, and went down to our meeting room with a cup of coffee and a blueberry muffin. The atmosphere in the meeting room was super intense. You could have cut it with a knife. *What the hell is going on?* I asked myself. I took a seat anticipating a normal pregame meeting for our 11:30 kickoff. The referee generally guides the meeting and everyone has input during the time we are together.

About fifteen minutes into our meetings, things came to a screeching halt. Buddy Patey was our observer, assigned from the conference office. He was an older, retired SEC veteran official and a pretty good guy. The look on his face showed that he was as clueless as I about what was going on.

275

The referee exclaimed, "We've got to clear the air and get ready to work this ballgame!" Over the next thirty minutes, I started to become aware of what I had missed the day before due to my flight delay. After the game, I learned everything that had gone on the day before.

On Friday evening, six crewmembers went on to Doe's Eat Place without Mike Wallace and me. Mike had also been delayed but not by much. He would just go directly to the restaurant from the airport. When Mike landed, he called the referee and told him that he was on his way. This official offered to go ahead and place Mike's order for him. Mike Wallace was your prototypical umpire. In other words, he was a big ole boy. This is when the weekend began to spiral out of control.

Mike told the referee what type and size of steak he wanted, along with his preferred side items. When Mike finished, he was told, "You don't need to eat all that!" *Oh, shit.* You don't say that to Mike.

Mike got to the restaurant and gave everyone a piece of his mind. He then began to eat. A couple of the guys tried to smooth things over with Mike. The other four finished and decided to drive on back to the hotel, figuring Mike would bring these two guys with him. Wrong.

When Mike finished dinner, he went out to his car and drove to the hotel alone. It had started to rain, so the referee and the line judge had to walk back in the rain. This was pre-Uber and there were no cabs available.

The referee has very thin hair on the top of his head and, supposedly, when he arrived back at the hotel, he looked like a drowned rat. The other guy was soaked, as well.

It took a while for Mike to get checked in. However, this delay coincided perfectly with the walker's arrival back to the hotel and their entering the elevator.

Mike and the other two crewmates ended up in the same elevator. The referee comes unglued and jumps up into Mike's face. He is *NOT* a "big ole boy." In fact, next to Mike, he looks pretty small. Fortunately, Mike restrained himself and no blows were exchanged. Everyone went to their room really pissed off.

When it was time for the referee to come and pick me up, he asked one of the other guys to come ride with him. The road out to the airport is very dark and curvy. He wanted some company.

So, after our early game on Saturday, which was uneventful, I realized why I got the response about the warm beer that I did. I had missed the whole "battle royale"!

YOU BETTER BEHAVE

During the 2005 and 2006 seasons, Steve Patrick was the back judge on our crew. Steve lived in Birmingham, Alabama, at that time. He later moved a little farther into north Alabama.

Steve was one of those guys that I connected with and picked on from time to time. We had an ongoing threat that one day, we were going to go to the middle of the field, right on the home-team logo, and get after it until only one person walked away. Our objective: to win an ESPY, the coveted award presented by ESPN.

While working in a late-season game at Arkansas, Steve was really giving me grief during the team's warm-up period. Since it was their homecoming game, I decided to be one of the officials to voluntarily go out and monitor the players to make sure no one got out of hand. Plus, homecoming always brings out the pretty women.

Who I should have been looking out for was "Little Patrick." That's how I referred to him. For some reason, he was giving me an extra dose of aggravation this particular afternoon.

Steve's dad, Bob Patrick, was officiating in the league when I started. Bob and I worked several games together in the early part of my career. When he retired from the SEC, Bob put me in his spot officiating the Senior Bowls that were played in Mobile, Alabama. This was a rite of passage that I appreciate to this day.

The fact that his dad was an official, coupled with the fact that Steve was not very tall, helped create his nickname.

Once, while working a Sun Bowl game with Steve in El

Paso, Texas, our crew was taken to a western boot store. Just about everyone in the group bought at least one pair. Over the next two days, Steve went on and on about how the deal he got on his boots was the best of anybody else's. It got to the point where enough was enough. Finally, I pointed out to him, and everyone else standing around, that little kid boots cost a lot less than full-grown men boots. We never heard anything more about how cheap his boots were.

Back to the Arkansas game: While Steve's antagonizing me while walking around on the field, I spot one of the most authentic-looking Santa Clauses sitting in the stands. I point him out to Steve and say, "Hey, Little Patrick, if you don't start acting right, Santa's not going to bring you anything for Christmas!" That one statement evened us up for the things he had been saying to me over the previous hour.

Steve moved on to officiate in the NFL and he continues doing so as of this writing.

I'VE GOT AN INTERPRETER

Being invited to speaking engagements and talking about college football is one of the most enjoyable things I get to do. In the South, it's a natural topic for most people.

My style may be a little different than most people, but it has worked well for over thirty years. I've used videos, PowerPoint presentations, props of various design, and I always try to weave in a couple of jokes along the way.

Lately, I only take a few notes with me that are typed on my cell phone. I hit a few high points and move the presentation to a question-and-answer period as quickly as possible. Doing presentations this way keeps the audience engaged. As a presenter, losing the interest of the attendees is an awkward experience. It's possible to get them back, but most of the time, you must abandon your outline.

I anticipate the same types of questions at every event. I also brush up on any high-profile incidents or game situations that may have occurred during the previous weekend. There may have been a play in a game that needs clarification regarding a rule application. A quick scan of any major sports publication will let me know what I needed to research.

While I was an active official, I would begin my presentations by telling the audience that there will be some questions that I cannot answer due to my relationship with the SEC. It was important to me to let them know that in advance so that they shouldn't take anything personally if I didn't answer their questions.

My thoughts on coaches were one of these questions that I

would skirt around. It was not a good idea to let my feelings about certain coaches become public. Yes, I had opinions, but I chose to keep those private. However, there would be some general questions that I felt comfortable talking about concerning these men.

During the 2019 season, LSU was rolling. I had a couple of games with them, both in Baton Rouge. Because their team was so good and ultimately ended up winning the national championship, I would be asked questions concerning them.

The head coach at LSU during this season was Ed Orgeron. I first got to know him when he was hired to be the head coach at Ole Miss from 2005 to 2007. Coach O was a great guy to work with on the sidelines.

As the LSU questions were asked, I would evaluate them and provide an appropriate answer that would keep me out of trouble. Most questions were able to be answered objectively.

During one question and answer period, I called on a lady near the back of the room we were in. She started out by saying she had seen Coach Orgeron during a postgame interview and had a hard time understanding what he was saying due to his Louisiana dialect. Then she asked her question, "Can you understand him during the game?"

Then came my answer.

"Yes, ma'am. The Southeastern Conference office has enough resources so that whenever you are scheduled to work a game with LSU, they provide an interpreter to go with you."

THE SLIM JIM

I've spoken to civic organizations, teacher groups, schools, business seminars, alumni associations, and even during church services. The number of the people in attendance ranged from ten to over eight hundred. I was never nervous during these gatherings nor did these engagements require much in the way of preparation. It's easy to get up and talk about something that people are really interested in. You don't have to use all the social engagement tools to keep people interested when you're talking about college football in the South.

One part of my presentation that I kept consistent was always asking a rules question with the promise of a special prize to the person that provided the correct answer. In over two hundred talks around the country, I was never given the correct answer.

Since the prize was never awarded, it was never revealed to the audience.

During the summer of 2022, I was asked to make a presentation at the College Football Hall of Fame in downtown Atlanta. If you ever get a chance to visit, do it. You can spend all day there and still not see it all. While getting dressed, I put on one of my favorite sport coats. My special prize was still hidden inside the left-breast pocket. I'm not sure what the life expectancy of a Slim Jim is but it's still available to the person providing the correct answer.

SUSTENANCE, OR LACK THEREOF

Officials arrive at the stadium no later than two hours and thirty minutes prior to the start of their game. The drive to the stadium averages fifteen minutes. After adding the average game time and the return trip to the hotel, you have a total time span of six hours and fifteen minutes. That's the minimum length of time from leaving the hotel and returning back to it.

No matter the time of kickoff, a meal is going to be missed. Around the SEC, there is no consistency from school to school on what is made available for the officials to eat. Some places do better than others. A couple of places are embarrassingly terrible at it.

At the bottom of the list is Vanderbilt. When you get to the tiny room they provide for the officials, there is a small refrigerator with a padlock on it. A room monitor comes in after everyone arrives and removes the lock. Inside are soft drinks. That's it for the next six-plus hours. To offset this, officials have conditioned themselves to bring a loaf of bread, along with peanut butter and jelly. They also carry a knife or spoon with them.

I'd put Texas A&M at next to the bottom of the list. Along with soft drinks, they do offer sports drinks and packs of nuts and protein bars. The real drawback there is that you share the locker room with some other people, whose purpose I never figured out. They were more of a pain in the ass to us. Maybe they were just boosters who had put in enough money. They wore officiating pants and white polo-type shirts.

Georgia is going into the number-three slot from the bottom. They offer a white shoebox with a cold ham-and-cheese sandwich, an apple, along with a chocolate-chip cookie.

The next ten schools are pretty much the same. They offer trays of fruit and vegetables, sliced meats, a couple of different types of bread, along with a variety of beverages. Some places like Kentucky offer coffee and hot chocolate.

In my opinion, the school at the top of the list is South Carolina. First, the officials' locker room has several leather couches and sofa chairs. It's spacious. There's plenty of beverages. But the food is far and away the best in the league.

There are enough boxed lunches for each official to have two: one for their time at the stadium and one to take with them back to the hotel.

Inside each box is a fried chicken breast, potato salad, a hard-boiled egg, a bag of potato chips, and to top it off, a delicious piece of pecan pie. Believe it or not, I had a fellow official tell me that he didn't like pecan pie. I replied, "Good, I'll eat it!" almost before he got the words out of his mouth.

PERSONALIZED HOTDOGS

In 2002, I had a day game at Tennessee. It was a weird start time, like five p.m. eastern time. Far enough away from lunch and too soon for dinner. When we arrived at the stadium around 2:30, I was starving. Each home school sends in a liaison to check on the officials after their arrival to see if they need anything. I asked the guy if there was anywhere that I could get something to eat. He told me that he would find something and bring it back to me. Just give him a few minutes.

Sure enough, he came back about fifteen minutes later with three Hebrew National hotdogs. He even thought to bring packages of ketchup and mustard.

When he brought them in, his counterpart with Alabama, "Red," observed from an adjacent room waiting for the pregame conference to begin. The hotdogs were really good and got me through the game.

Three weeks later, I'm in Tuscaloosa for a game. When the crew arrives in our room at Bryant-Denny Stadium, Red comes in to check on us. Without saying a word, he hands me three hotdogs. He was not going to be outdone by Tennessee.

For almost twenty years, whenever I had a game at Alabama or Tennessee, there were always at least three hot dogs in the officials' dressing room, with my name on them!

OH GOD!

Playing practical jokes on fellow crew members is like a rite of passage. As you get to know people, and after spending a lot of time with them, information is obtained to maximize the effectiveness of administering grief upon them.

For instance, Russ Pulley loves to eat. He will plan his entire day around it. When we were working together, over the course of a couple of seasons, he would look forward to eating once he arrived at the stadium for our game.

Russ was a really good official. He was tall, athletic and had big feet—*enormous* feet. When he set his mind on something, he was laser focused.

During a game in Gainesville, Florida, he knew he was going to eat once he got to our locker room. The people at Florida put a lot of really good food in the room for us to eat. There was fresh fruit and bread. The sliced meat was always fresh and there was plenty of it. There was cheese and condiments. You ate well, and you could eat healthy at the same time.

During our pregame meeting, Russ talked about waiting to have lunch once we got to the stadium. On our drive over, he continued to remind everyone that he would be eating. Once we parked outside the doors to walk to our room, I hurried ahead of everyone else. Russ brought up the rear.

As soon as I entered the room, I stacked up all the trays and took them into the restroom area. I opened one of the stall doors and put them on the lid of the toilet. I then went back and sat on one of the couches in the room.

Russ was the last one to enter the room. He went straight to the table that now lay bare. He stood there and only muttered,

"Oh, God! There's no food." Everyone was thinking the same thing. *How come there's no food?* I let this play out for about five minutes and walked into the restroom.

When I returned to the room, with trays of food in hand, Russ was like a kid on Christmas morning. Everyone, including Steve Shaw, our serious referee, thought it was hysterical. If you can't pick on people, including yourself, you don't need to officiate in the SEC.

Acknowledgments

While writing this book, it has become crystal clear just how many blessings God has placed before me. He has given me two children whom I admire more and more each day. He has provided me with good health. He has laid before me a patchwork of experiences through life that are unimaginable in hindsight. Without him, I wouldn't have the ability to remember those experiences, much less be able to share them on paper. The sense of humor he has given me helps while navigating the difficulties we all face.

There are the hundreds of officials, coaches, players, and staff members who provided the story material along my journey. Each and every one I came across during my career left a lasting impression. Without them, these stories wouldn't exist.

If not for the suggestion from my friend Stan Ryals, I wouldn't have started a list of story reminders just in case the day came where I would consider actually writing a book. Two years and almost 350 story titles later, it was time.

My incredible team at BookLogix. Writing a book is a grueling task, particularly for a rookie author. The wonderful people at BookLogix made the process much easier than I ever imagined possible. Thank you!

Especially my son and daughter, August and Susan, for reminding me that life is always beginning. While writing this book, they are preparing themselves for parenting and marriage, respectively. Hopefully, I was able to provide you with some skills that will help you sail through your own journeys.

About the Author

G. A. "Gus" Morris III was born and raised in Atlanta, Georgia, where he played multiple youth sports. After graduating from Millsaps College, he was inducted into their Hall of Fame as a football player. After his playing days, Gus used football officiating for recreation and to remain physically active. In 2021, he retired from officiating college football in the Southeastern Conference after an incredible thirty-one-year career that includes five SEC Championships, sixteen postseason bowl games, seven Senior Bowls, and two Blue-Grey All-Star games.

In this wonderful piece of storytelling, Gus shares his experiences that will make you laugh, cry, and realize what it takes to be an official at the highest levels.

His time away from the gridiron is now filled with serving on the boards of several nonprofit organizations, mentoring young officials, and spending time in the outdoors with his Vizslas, Reagan and Eunice.

Saturdays in the South is Gus's first book.